THE CONCEPT OF PEACE

John Macquarrie

THE CONCEPT OF
PEACE

The Firth Lectures, 1972

SCM PRESS LTD

172.4

334 00260 5

First published 1973
by SCM Press Ltd
56 Bloomsbury Street London

© SCM Press Ltd 1973

Photoset and Printed
by Redwood Press Limited
Trowbridge, Wiltshire

IN MEMORY OF
DONALD M. SWANSON

CONTENTS

PREFACE

I wish to thank the trustees of the Firth Lectureship for the honour which they did me in inviting me to deliver the Firth Lectures in the University of Nottingham in 1972. I wish also to thank the officers of the University and the members of the Theology Department for the many kindnesses which they showed me on my visits to Nottingham. I am indebted to Professor Ronald Preston for some useful criticisms and suggestions.

Christ Church, Oxford   John Macquarrie

ONE

Peace: Technique and Concept

Some years ago I wrote that 'peace is the most inclusive of Christian virtues' and went on to urge that 'a Christian ethic for our time may profitably devote much more attention than has been given in the past to the exploration of this great biblical idea of peace and the ways to its realization'.[1] The present book is an attempt to take up the task announced in that earlier writing.

One good reason for giving to peace the paramount place among the Christian virtues is just the indisputable fact that in the contemporary world the lives of all people are bound together in an interdependence closer and more evident than has ever been known before. The corporate nature of human existence is daily being impressed upon us. No individual, no group, no nation can contract out of the human family or isolate itself from the rest. The destinies of those who inhabit this closely-knit planet are now seen to be as inseparable as the destinies of a group of travellers on a space-ship. It follows, then, that our ethical thinking must be guided by a conception of a virtue that is corporate or even global in its scope, and such a virtue is peace.

Traditionally, of course, the three principal Christian virtues were reckoned to be faith, hope and love. But these are qualities which we associate more readily with the life of the individual than with the life of society. Even love, the crown of the Christian life, is usually considered as a relation between individuals. Of course, the word 'love' – like the word 'peace' – is commonly used far too glibly and without proper consideration of its deeper meanings, so that to think of love primarily in individual terms may be simply a failure to grasp its full height and breadth and length and depth. Nonetheless, if the conditions of our time are demanding that we think in corporate terms, then it is arguable that we should see the crown of the Christian life in the unquestionably corporate virtue of peace.

It need hardly be said that peace and love are in no sense rivals for the primacy in the moral life. It would be more correct to say that peace is love transposed into social or global terms. Yet such a statement would have to be qualified by the recognition that the relation between an individual virtue and a social virtue is a very complex one. In discussing the nature of justice, Plato claimed that justice in the state is like large writing on a large surface, and so easier to discern than justice in the individual, said to be like small writing seen at a distance.[2] But it could be argued that the social expression of the virtue is more complex and more difficult to understand. In the case with which we are concerned, peace implies justice as well as love. It is not simply a transposing of an individual virtue into a social medium, but a gathering together of many virtues and their transmutation on to a new level of complexity.

This last remark will also make it clear that the recommendation to give greater attention to the corporate virtues cannot mean that one neglects or despises the individual virtues. If traditional Christianity (especially of the evangelical and pietistic sort) laid too much stress on individual sanctification, traditional Marxism fell into the opposite mistake of supposing that the good life for man could be realized through the transformation of social structures. An exploration of the meaning of peace will show the inadequacy of both points of view, for while peace is primarily a corporate virtue, it implies also an integrity at the individual level.

Peace is an obvious theme for Christian-Marxist dialogue, for both Christians and Marxists claim to be concerned about peace. But not only Christians and Marxists are concerned about peace. So too are Buddhists and humanists, people of many religions and many ideologies. Peace is of urgent concern to all mankind. This is another good reason for making it the central concept in a discussion of Christian ethics, for it stresses the continuity of Christian goals and aspirations with those for which all men of good will are striving. Although the discussion of peace in this book is undertaken from the point of view of biblical faith and Christian theology, it is hoped that it will commend itself to non-Christians also as a contribution to a theme that is of vital interest to all. And this does not simply mean trying to establish the 'relevance' of Christianity to the human predicament. Rather, it is taking seriously the fact that Christians are involved in that solidarity of the human race mentioned earlier, and that peace, if it is ever to be achieved, must be a co-operative venture cutting across all faiths and ideologies. Indeed, if one thinks of some of the leading protagonists of peace in recent decades, they represent many forms of belief and unbelief – Mohandas Gandhi, Bertrand Russell, George Bell, Martin Luther King, Dag Hammarskjöld, to mention only a few.

How does one make a beginning towards understanding the nature of peace? No doubt there are several possible starting-points. But one way which will impress us both with the urgency and with the enormous complexity of the subject is to consider the many ways in which human life is fractured. All of us have experience of at least some of these fractured areas. It is at such points that the need and longing for peace arise. When I use the word 'fracture', I mean that a real break has occurred, and that conflict, which is not necessarily in itself a bad thing, has escalated to the point at which the conflicting parties can no longer communicate with each other and seek only to coerce one another. There is more or less total alienation and estrangement, and this can still be very destructive even if it does not issue in overt violence.

War between nations is the most obvious and most destructive of all the fractures that occur in the life of mankind. Large-scale international wars have now reached such a pitch of destructiveness that the great powers are unlikely to launch such wars, though one might begin by accident. But even if a world war of the kind which broke out in 1914 and 1939 seems unthinkable today, war itself is still with us. During the past two or three decades, there has usually been a so-called 'limited' war going on somewhere – in Korea, the Middle East, the Indian sub-continent, Indo-China – and such limited wars are often far more destructive of life and property than were so-called 'major' wars of the past. The pattern of a war is significant. Diplomatic relations are broken off and ambassadors recalled. This is the breakdown of communication, the stage of total alienation. Then nothing remains but force, and this may escalate to the extremes of violence.

As well as national wars, there are also civil wars and varying degrees of civil strife and violence that may fall short of actual war. There is something peculiarly horrifying about these domestic forms of strife – and I speak as one who has seen something of this at first hand, both in North Africa and North America. People who may have been long neighbours are suddenly in a state of total alienation and are driven to quite untypical acts of violence by mingled fear and hostility. The causes of such strife are various. Differences of religion and language can still lead to riots and bloodshed, even in relatively sophisticated European countries; for instance, in Ireland Protestants and Catholics still fight it out, while in

4

Belgium sporadic violence still erupts between Flemish speakers and French speakers. But far more potent are racial and
economic differences, often combined in the same situation.
The most potentially dangerous situations in the world today
are those in which there exist racial differences aligned with
great economic and social inequalities.

We usually think of war, in one or other of its forms, as the
opposite of peace, but wherever human life is fractured, peace
has been destroyed. Industry is an area of human life where
bitter divisions take place. We are familiar with the expression
'industrial peace', but for much of the time it represents an
aspiration rather than a reality. The strike and lock-out have
the same formal pattern as war – a breakdown of communication followed by attempted coercion. Though money is
often the ostensible cause of industrial unrest, most analysts of
the problem are agreed that the causes lie much deeper.
Already in the early decades of the industrial revolution Hegel
was pointing to a form of alienation that was arising in
people's work.[3] Man had always been a tool user, but the tool
is like an extension of his own body, so that in using the tool
one is scarcely aware of it, for attention is fixed on the object
of one's work. But with the coming of the machine, a change
takes place. As Hegel puts it, the machine 'works for' man,
that is to say, it interposes itself between man and the object of
his work. His attention may now be taken up with the
machine itself to ensure that it runs efficiently, and he may
think of himself increasingly as superfluous. With Marx, the
notion of alienation in work is given a further dimension. Man
has become himself a commodity, to be bought and sold, hired
and fired. He is alienated not only from the product of his
work but even from himself. Although we have moved far
from the conditions of work that prevailed in the days of
Hegel and Marx, the problems remain. Indeed, the vast technological apparatus of the contemporary world has acquired

an independence and momentum of its own, so that sometimes it appears that no one can control it any more, and the individual worker may well feel himself alienated from the entire system. Certainly there are fractures in the world of work and industry that bring about a very profound unease and unrest.

Marriage and the family constitute another area of human life in which there are deep fractures. To be sure, the 'war of the sexes' is nothing new, and neither is the generation gap, and these may be considered as respectively the horizontal and the vertical strains that are experienced in every marriage and family situation. Such tensions in themselves can be healthy and creative. But they can also come to the breaking point, where communication ceases and the parties face each other in uncomprehending hostility. It would seem that in our own time the danger of fracturing, both vertical and horizontal, is increased by factors operating in contemporary society. High mobility and transience begin to affect not only our relation to things and places but to persons, and militate against any profound permanent relationship, even in marriage; while the sheer rapidity of social and technological change exacerbates the generation gap to the point where parents and children are living almost in different worlds.

Up to this point we have been considering divisions among people, the alienation of races, nations, economic groups and so on. But there are other fractures too and these, as we shall see, have a relation to the question of peace.

Man has always been involved in a struggle with nature. It has been a hard battle, but also a bracing and invigorating one. But that battle has become in recent times an all-out war. Armed with his new scientific technology, man is winning that war in a way that would once have seemed impossible. Nature is more and more subjected to man's will and its treasures are more and more at his disposal. But we have become aware that this may turn out to have been a hollow victory. The environmental crisis is already upon us, and even if one does not go along with the most gloomy forecasts, it would be the height of irresponsibility to ignore sober warnings or to believe blindly that further refinements in technology will solve the problems. Full exploitation of natural resources and increase of the human population are ends for which men long battled against nature; but now that they are within our grasp, they are proving to be mixed blessings, whilst such side-effects as pollution hint at dangers the extent of which is still unknown. It seems clear that we need to make our peace with nature and to come to a *modus vivendi*. But unfortunately, the war between man and nature is aggravating some of those fractures and divisions that exist between men themselves. While the technologically advanced countries are talking about the limits to growth and are seeking to impose stricter controls on technological development, the undeveloped countries are planning for industrialization and the affluence which they hope it will bring. The question of how man can live at peace with nature is not therefore separable from questions of international and economic justice.

We may push our survey of the fractures in human life back to the individual. As well as being divided from his fellow human beings or from the environing nature, man may be divided within himself. The human self has a very complicated structure, something of which we can express by saying that a man has a relation to himself. He may be at one with himself, or he may be divided in himself. In this connection we find the expressions 'peace' and 'war' being used again. We can say of a person that he is at peace with himself, or that he enjoys an inward peace. On the other hand, we sometimes say that someone is at war with himself. There is a spectrum stretching all the way from the person who is, as we say, well integrated to those pathological conditions in which the self has become fragmented. Presumably everyone at some time or another

7

knows inward conflict, and this may be intense. Like the other forms of conflict we have considered, this is not in itself necessarily bad, and may even be essential to the development of a mature person. But here too there is the danger that the conflict may deepen to the point where a real fracture occurs. Freud went so far as to claim that there are two fundamental instincts in man, a positive instinct oriented towards the expansion and enhancement of life, and a negative or destructive instinct which leads back from life to the non-living.[4] If this is so, then the seeds of war and destruction lie very deep in every individual human person. One may still ask, however, whether one or other of these instincts, Eros or Thanatos, is more primordial than its opposite. We leave aside this question for the present. It is enough for the moment to note that one dimension of the problem of peace reaches deeply into the personal life of the individual. For that life can itself be seriously fractured, and the quest for peace is inward as well as outward.

There is still another area of human life where both fracturing and the quest for peace are known – the theological area. 'Peace' is a word that is common in the vocabularies of many religions, but there it refers to man's relation, not to his fellows or to nature or even to himself, but to the ultimate reality which religion names God. To enjoy peace in the religious sense is to be at home in the world and to have a sense of affinity and perhaps a hope or confidence in the underlying reality of the world. But in modern times this area too is fractured. God or the gods, as they were once conceived, seem to have withdrawn. The world in the past few centuries has come to appear more and more as a godless, impersonal, mechanical, faceless reality, indifferent and even oppressive to man. Nietzsche's saying that God is dead brings to expression the sense of alienation and isolation experienced by man in the face of a vast cosmos which, he begins to suspect, may have neither beginning nor end nor centre, neither direction nor meaning. Much of the most sensitive literature of modern times has expressed this deep feeling of alienation from reality itself. Kafka's *The Castle* is a classic example; the heart of things is cold, impersonal, anonymous, unintelligible. The kind of peace and sense of affinity which men once enjoyed seems broken. Yet the fracture itself seems to have stirred up a new quest for this most ultimate kind of peace. There is a new wave of religious questing among the young, while in literature too there is a movement beyond alienation. Commenting on this aspect of modern literature, Nathan Scott claims that 'the world must somehow be found once again to be not a static universe of inert fact but an environment available on the terms of intimacy and offering the possibility of a participatory relationship . . . The inchoate yearning that seems to have captured many of the most sensitive people of our age, if given a theological formulation, might be said to be a yearning to behold the world as once again a truly sacramental economy'.[5]

Our brief survey of what I have called the 'fractured areas' of life and the many-sided quest for peace that tries to reach across these fractures has made clear how vast and complex the problem of peace is. It has also made clear how complex and multi-dimensional is the concept of peace, if it is to be at all adequate to the human situation and if we are to think of it in any depth. Peace has to be conceived in a sufficiently comprehensive way to embrace all the interlocking problems that we have passed in review.

All this means that peace has an intellectual aspect. It demands intellectual effort, and it demands knowledge. All the goodwill in the world will never establish peace without hard thinking. In this respect at least, peace is like love. In his splendid study of love, Daniel D. Williams points out that 'it is the sheerest sentimentality to suppose that love can dispense

9

with objective knowledge', and later he says that 'intellect needs love, and love needs intellectual understanding'.[6] One might make exactly the same affirmation about peace. Peace cannot dispense with objective knowledge – indeed, it demands a vast store of such knowledge, such as could be supplied by a whole host of experts in many different fields. But it cannot dispense either with an intellectual understanding of what peace essentially is. It is a pity that although there is a universal longing for peace and sometimes enthusiastic demonstrations for peace, it is not always appreciated that these are doomed to futility unless they are matched by an intellectual grasp of the problem.

But this in itself is a complex matter. I have mentioned two aspects of it – objective knowledge and an intellectual grasp of peace itself.

The first of these two aspects is one which no one will be disposed to deny. Peace is, in one aspect, a technique, or rather a whole set of intermeshing techniques. This became plain enough in our survey of those areas where human life is fractured and the search for peace arises. If peace is ever to be built, it can only come about through the co-operative strivings of those who possess a technical knowledge and expertise in the many fields that in one way or another have their relevance to the quest for peace. Clearly, the politician skilled in statecraft has an important role. But so has the economist who knows about the production and distribution of goods. So have scientists of many kinds, men with understanding of the problems of food supply, public health and the like. So have psychologists and sociologists, especially those skilled in promoting good relations between individuals and between groups with divergent interests. Perhaps a special importance belongs to educationists in helping to form peaceful attitudes. One could expand the list almost indefinitely. Peace in the modern world needs to harness all the technical skills that abound today.

One must not for a moment underrate the importance of the techniques of peace, the objective knowledge of one kind or another which is essential to the realization of peace and which is scattered through many groups of specialists. But while acknowledging this, one must also be clear that another kind of knowledge is needed too, and needed just as urgently. This I have called 'an intellectual grasp of what peace essentially is'. It is the concept of peace. This is something of a different order from the technical knowledge we have been considering. We need also the distinctive contribution of the reflective disciplines, and among these I include Christian theology which offers, I believe, a uniquely rich and comprehensive concept of peace.

But do we really need anything of the sort? There is a tendency nowadays to believe that all problems are really technical problems, and are to be solved by techniques. And correspondingly there is suspicion of the theologian or the metaphysician or the reflective type of philosopher, all of whom may seem to be remote from the social and material forces that are really shaping our world.

But against such a position it has to be pointed out first that techniques and objective knowledge do not themselves establish the values or determine the goals for which men strive. The resources of psychology and modern educational methods can be and sometimes are used for propaganda purposes and can be as effective in the service of hatred as of peace. We need a concept of peace of sufficient depth and persuasiveness to exert a purchase on human aspirations and to provide direction and motivation for our techniques. We need an ethical vision of a truly personal and truly fulfilling human community, and such a vision is not a product of any technique, though it needs techniques for its realization. Furthermore, we have been learning in recent times the dangers that attend the fragmentation of knowledge and effort in a society of highly specialized expertise. It was the strength of Western man that he could isolate limited, manageable problems and then develop the special knowledge and skills to deal with them. But this is proving to be also a weakness, for we have not been sufficiently able to see things in their wholeness or to coordinate the manifold operations of a modern industrial society. The most obvious illustration of this is the environmental problem. An adequate concept of peace could well act as a kind of focus on which the divergent concerns might converge. We have said that peace must, on the one hand, be a vast co-operative venture; but how can that co-operation take place unless there is a common focus or goal, a concept of peace that brings together and unifies the many separate endeavours?

Although for the most part I have used the expression 'concept of peace', I have also used the word 'vision'. One may speak both of the Christian concept of peace and of the Christian vision of peace, but there is a difference between these expressions. When one speaks of the vision of peace, one has in mind its ideal character. To use more definitely theological language, peace, as Christian faith conceives it, has an eschatological character. It belongs to the end, to the fulfilled goal of creation. Presumably it can never be fully realized under historical conditions, and so there are in it elements of mystery and transcendence. Of course, peace in any worthwhile sense is a long-term goal. Even if all wars and violence throughout the world were to cease tomorrow, there would still be generations of work ahead before the fractures of human society could be healed and the many alienations overcome. The peace of the Christian vision is not only long-term but eschatological, a peace of such depth and comprehensiveness that it can only lie at the consummation of history.

However, I have deliberately laid stress on the Christian concept of peace rather than the vision. The trouble about a vision, and especially an eschatological vision, is that it can become so distant and so idealized that it no longer makes contact with one's actual situation or has any real purchase on one's present policies of action. In speaking of a concept of peace, I want to make the vision more definite and to relate it to our actual situation. A concept implies recognizable and describable structures, and these do belong to peace as Christian faith has understood it. Through seeking to understand these structures, the vision is brought out of its transcendent eschatological setting, and begins to exert a pressure on our immediate policies. An eschatological idea remains impotent and can even be a distraction if it is left isolated on the horizon of history; but it can be a powerful formative influence if it is conceptually related to actual historical situations. The double significance of peace as both vision and concept has been well expressed by J. Edward Barrett: 'The universal realization of peace is certainly not an immediate possibility. But the relative and proximate increase of peace is in every moment a very realistic possibility.'[7] In the next chapter we shall try to understand more clearly the nature of peace in biblical and Christian thought.

NOTES

1. John Macquarrie, *Three Issues in Ethics*, SCM Press 1970, p.66.

2. Plato, *The Republic*, 368.

3. G.W.F. Hegel, *The Phenomenology of Mind*, tr. J.B. Baillie, Allen and Unwin 1931, pp.500ff.

4. S. Freud, *An Outline of Psychoanalysis*, tr. James Strachey, Hogarth Press 1949, pp.5ff.

5. Nathan A. Scott, *The Wild Prayer of Longing*, Yale University Press 1971, p.40.

6. Daniel D. Williams, *The Spirit and Forms of Love*, Harper and Row 1969, pp.121,279.

7. J. Edward Barrett, *How Are You Programmed?*, John Knox Press 1971, p.84.

TWO

Peace and Human Nature

We turn now to the task of exploring in more detail the meaning of peace. I shall begin with some linguistic considerations. Language is like a museum, for the forms of the words which we use may still enable us to see how people began to think of the phenomena which these words signify, and this may give us an interesting glimpse into some of their basic convictions about man himself and about the kind of world in which he has to live his life. This is specially true in the case of words which stand for abstract ideas and which are usually derived from words denoting concrete objects or activities. It is instructive to study the words used in several languages for 'peace', as these reveal that already at a prephilosophical level there were important differences as to what peace really is.

Let us consider first the Hebrew word, since this is important for the whole biblical tradition. That Hebrew word is *shalom*, and the basic meaning which the dictionary assigns to it is 'completeness' or 'wholeness.'[1] The noun *shalom* is derived from the verbal form, *shalem*, which, in its various possible forms, can mean 'to be complete', 'to make complete' or 'to finish', even 'to make an end of'. Thus, when the word *shalom* is used for peace, what those who used it originally had in view was a condition of the world or of human society in which there is completeness, unity, wholeness, fullness. All these words which I have used to express the meaning of peace as *shalom* are thoroughly affirmative words. Where there is peace, both the whole and its constituent parts have reached their maximal and optimal levels of being. Another language possessing a word for peace having somewhat similar connotations is Russian. The single word *mir* can in modern Russian do duty for both 'peace' and 'world'. Although etymologically there were two distinct words, their convergence and the exploitation of this convergence is quite understandable. A world is something complete or whole. The peace of the world would be simply the true worldhood of the world, and a world at peace would be a world which had really grown to the maturity of that wholeness which the notion of 'world' is intended to convey. Sanskrit and the Indian languages derived from it also illustrate an affirmative way of understanding peace. *Santi* means spiritual contentment, a profound integration of the inward life of man.

In contrast to the Semitic, Slavonic and Indian words just considered, the words for peace used in the classical languages of Western Europe have mostly a negative significance. Peace is seen as the absence or suspension of strife. Concerning the Greek word for peace, *eirene*, a lexicographer writes: 'The basic feature of the Greek concept of *eirene* is that the word does not primarily denote a relationship between several people or an attitude, but a state of affairs, a time of peace or a state of peace, originally conceived of purely as an interlude in the everlasting state of war.'[2] *Eirene* was basically a truce, whatever new meanings the word may have acquired in the course of its history. The Latin word *pax* is somewhat different, yet fundamentally it seems to indicate a basically similar way of understanding the human condition. *Pax* is an agreement or compact. It is not a primary wholeness or concord, but a secondary state of affairs, a more or less fragile agreement established in the course of the unremitting struggle between conflicting interests. These words then, *eirene* and *pax*, disclose through their semantic origins a very different pre-philosophical understanding of the essence of peace from the one which is to be seen underlying the words *shalom* and *santi*.

The Chinese language seems to offer a third possibility. The word for peace, *ping*, means in its verbal sense 'to adjust', 'to weigh in the balance', 'to harmonize'. Here the idea seems to be neither wholeness nor cessation of conflict, but rather a diversity in unity, or the taking up of conflict into a kind of equilibrium of forces. This introduces a dynamic element into the understanding of peace, and this is important, as we shall see in due course. The notion of the *yin* and the *yang*, the negative and positive forces whose interaction and mutual adjustments determine historical and cosmic happenings, is, of course, very ancient in Chinese thought. But something of the doctrine persists in the contemporary Chinese understanding of Marxism. According to Mao Tse-Tung, 'Marxist philosophy holds that the law of the unity of opposites is the fundamental law of the universe.' However, we must note that he adds: 'In any given phenomenon or thing, the unity of opposites is conditional, temporary and transitory, and hence relative, whereas the struggle of opposites is absolute.'[3] Thus he seems to come down finally on the side of those who see struggle as the basic condition.

Although I have spent a little time in this discussion of some of the words for peace used in the major languages of mankind, and although I believe that some interest attaches to this discussion, I do not wish to lay too much stress on etymological considerations. Whatever the original meanings of words may have been, they often develop new meanings in the course of their histories, and the original meanings may be almost forgotten. Furthermore, linguistic considerations of the kind we have had before us show us only the pre-philosophical way of grasping and interpreting phenomena, and any discussion about different ways of grasping the essence of peace would need to be examined at the level of conscious reflective theories of man and society. Such an examination will in fact follow in due course,[4] though we shall find that the basic ways of conceiving peace at the pre-philosophical level reappear as sophisticated theories.

But first of all we return to the biblical notion of peace, *shalom*. We have already seen that the Hebrew word means 'wholeness' or 'completeness', so that the biblical understanding of the meaning of peace sets out with an affirmative bias. Peace is not merely cessation of strife, but a positive quality of individual and social life.

But the notion of wholeness remains in itself somewhat vague. I have spoken of peace as the 'inclusive' virtue. But if, as wholeness, it includes everything, then does it not become a very amorphous idea? It overlaps so many limited virtues and is concerned with so many areas of human life that it seems to be in danger of becoming an inflated ideal which has no clearly discernible relation to concrete ethical problems and offers little guidance for their solution.

An examination of the biblical teaching on peace does, however, reveal a definite structure. We have to do not just with a hazy vision but with a structured concept having identifiable features.

To be sure, the first characteristic which one must recognize in the biblical concept of peace is its eschatological nature. According to Isaiah, it will be 'in the latter days' that men will live together in peace according to law:

> 'And they shall beat their swords into ploughshares,
>   And their spears into pruning hooks;
> Nation shall not lift up sword against nation,
>   Neither shall they learn war any more.'[5]

This establishment of peace in the full sense will coincide with the realization of the messianic kingdom at the end time. One of the titles of the Messiah himself is 'Prince of Peace'.[6]

Yet there is a sense in which peace also belongs to the beginning; it was the original condition of man. C. F. Evans writes, concerning the Old Testament teaching: 'Peace is the normal and proper condition of men in relationship with one another.[7] The original condition of man was to live in paradise. This mythological conception does not mean that in the beginning there was some kind of Golden Age, nor is it an ancient version of the Enlightenment myth of the noble savage. It means that human nature is essentially a peaceable nature and fulfils itself in peace; and, conversely, that war is not man's natural condition but a corruption of his nature. To put the matter in a more theological way, the consummation of the kingdom of God at the end of history is made possible by the presence of the image of God at the beginning of history. Or to put the matter in still another, non-theological way, the final realization of peace among men as their highest fulfilment depends on the fact that peace has been the authentic potentiality for man ever since the distinctively human emerged on earth.

These points need to be forcibly made, because they are often obscured by an over-emphasis on the biblical doctrine of sin, and especially by a doctrine of original sin. Man is indeed in a sinful condition – we have seen the many ways in which his life is fractured. This sinfulness is, moreover, very deeply pervasive of man's life. Yet it must always be remembered that in biblical teaching righteousness is more original than sin. In Western Christianity there has been a tremendous emphasis on original sin, especially in such influential theologians as Augustine and Calvin. This, I think, has gone beyond the point of realism to an exaggeration which has tended to see human nature as essentially sinful. It is interesting to speculate whether there might be any connection between the pre-philosophical negative understanding of peace evinced in the Western vocabulary of *eirene* and *pax*, the heavy stress on original sin in Western theology, and the generally warlike and aggressive character of Western history. At any rate, in contradiction to this, the Bible considers righteousness more fundamental than sin, and so peace more fundamental than war.

We have seen that peace is, in biblical teaching, both eschatological and primordial. It is eschatological in the sense that its full realization belongs to the end of history. It is primordial in the sense that it was man's true potentiality from the beginning of his history. The essentially dynamic character of the biblical concept of peace emerges from this contrast. Peace is not simply a condition but a process and a task as man moves from potentiality to realization.

Although peace is presented in the Bible as an eschatological ideal, this does not mean that it is other-worldly or divorced from the life we know on earth. Especially in the Old Testament, peace is conceived in a thoroughly this-worldly way. So we must add as a further characteristic of the biblical understanding of peace that it includes material well-being. Man is an embodied creature and he cannot attain his full being as man if his bodily life and capacities are stunted. The prophet Zechariah writes: 'For there shall be a sowing of peace and prosperity; the vine shall yield its fruit, and the ground shall give its increase, and the heavens shall give their dew.'[8] Peace is therefore conceived as involving material abundance. Yet there is also a simplicity about this conception which marks it off from the acquisitiveness of a modern affluent society.

There is a related and very interesting strand in the Old Testament teaching about peace which has a bearing on our current preoccupation with ecology and with the question of how man can live at peace with nature. Some of the biblical writers visualize the final era of peace as one in which nature itself will be transformed. Or perhaps one should rather say that man's relation to nature will be transformed, and he will live in a new kind of symbiosis with nature. Ezekiel represents God as saying: 'I will make with them a covenant of peace and banish wild beasts from the land, so that they may dwell securely in the wilderness and sleep in the woods.'⁹ Isaiah envisages a time when 'the desert shall rejoice and blossom';¹⁰ or again, 'the wolf shall dwell with the lamb . . . they shall not hurt or destroy in all my holy mountain'.¹¹ Of course, this writing is poetic and visionary, yet it shows an awareness of the multiplicity of relationships that have to be transformed and renewed if man is ever to live in that wholeness which is his true peace.

Fundamental also to the Old Testament understanding of peace is justice. The prophets were the great protagonists of social justice, and again and again they condemn as a false peace any security that rests on oppression or is merely superficial. ' "There is no peace," says the Lord, "for the wicked." '¹² So peace is much more than the tranquil enjoyment of abundance. It requires its ethical just as much as its material aspect, and must be founded in justice.

In this discussion of the biblical material, I have so far dwelt mainly on the Old Testament writings, but peace is also an important conception in the New Testament. 'Peace I leave with you, my peace I give unto you,'¹³ is Jesus' legacy to his disciples, the summing up in a single concept of the whole meaning of his mission.

The close connection between the New Testament understanding of peace and Jesus' own person and work is expressed in the remarkable sentence, 'he is our peace'.¹⁴ Here Christ is simply identified with peace. Christ, however, is not to be understood as merely an individual man, Jesus of Nazareth. It is not as an isolated individual that Christ has significance, but as the manifestation of a new humanity. The sentence quoted, 'he is our peace', occurs in the context of a passage on the new human community that Christ was bringing into being. This was a community inseparable from him, and likewise he was inseparable from it. The reciprocal relationship is likened to that between head and body. The new community was a community of peace, for within it hitherto alienated groups, Jews and Gentiles, were coming together in a new unity. As the writer of this passage says, Christ 'has made us both one, and has broken down the dividing wall of hostility . . . that he might create in himself one new man in place of the two, so making peace'.[15]

By associating peace so closely with Christ himself and with the emerging Christian community, the New Testament adds a new dimension to the Old Testament teaching on this theme. There is on the one hand a deeper awareness of the resistance to peace, of the depth of alienation, 'the dividing wall of hostility' between rival groups of mankind. And with this goes a corresponding sense of the costliness of peace. It may be that peace is 'the normal and proper condition of men in relation to each other', but man's nature has been so perverted by sin and hostility has gained such a hold of his mind that peace can only be established by means of a costly reconciliation. Peace demands atonement, the making at one of those who have become separated. But atonement in turn means that a price has to be paid. If we come back for a moment to the passage from Ephesians which we have been considering, we must attend to these words of the writer: 'But now in Christ Jesus you who once were far off have been brought near in the blood of Christ.'[16] The members of that reconciled Christian community believed that the death of Christ, the shedding of his blood, had been the means of reconciliation. There have indeed been many attempts to work out a theology of atonement, some of them more and some of them less enlightening.

But what is of the essence of this teaching is the recognition that once they have become estranged through sin, human beings can be brought back into the proper relationship of peace only through a costly act of atonement. The death of Jesus Christ was such an act, but once again we must not isolate this event. Readiness to pay the price of peace must be found not only in Christ but in the reconciled community itself. This community must continue Christ's atoning work, it must 'complete what is lacking in Christ's afflictions'.[17] When Christ bequeathed the gift of peace to his followers and when as the climax of the beatitudes he commended the peacemakers,[18] we can see in retrospect that this was not the promise of tranquillity but the invitation to continue a costly work.

There is one remaining point that must be made in this delineation of the biblical concept of peace, namely, that the Old Testament and the New Testament are alike agreed that God himself is the final author of peace. The fullness of *shalom* is a divine gift. Actually there is a theological dimension in the different ways of understanding peace that we have observed even at the pre-philosophical level, as evidenced in the semantics of the words used for peace. On the negative view of peace as *pax*, conflict is primary and peace is an artificial construction designed to lessen the misery of unremitting conflict. On the affirmative view of peace as *shalom*, peace is primary and war is a falling away due to human sin. It is clear that on this second view (and it is here that the biblical concept belongs) one is placing a trust in human nature which is withheld on the first view. But there is even more to it. One is not only placing trust in human nature but one is also affirming that rationality is more fundamental than chaos. To trust human nature is in a manner to trust reality also, and this is at least part of what it means to believe in God. The full implications of this must be deferred for later consideration.

But meanwhile let us follow the two contrasting notions of

peace into the region of philosophical discussion. The negative view received perhaps its ablest expression in English philosophy from Thomas Hobbes.[19] According to him, the natural state of mankind is one of unrestricted war and competition. It is a war of every man against every man. In this state of war, nothing can be unjust, for there is no intrinsic standard of justice. Only human convention makes actions just or unjust. But in that natural state of war and competition, the life of man is, in the philosopher's famous words, 'solitary, poor, nasty, brutish and short'. The misery of such a way of life impels men to seek peace. According to Hobbes, 'the passions that incline men to peace are fear of death, desire of such things as are necessary to commodious living, and a hope by their industry to obtain them'. It is not necessary for us to follow his argument into the setting up of a commonwealth. The essential points are already before us, in the doctrine that man's natural condition is one of war and that peace is a secondary condition motivated by fear and by the inconvenience of perpetual struggle.

Hobbes' belief that struggle is the primary reality in human life has had many other advocates among philosophers and students of human nature. In the nineteenth century Carl von Clausewitz wrote an influential treatise on war in which he maintained that 'war is nothing but a continuation of political intercourse with a mixture of other means – merely another kind of writing and language for political thought'.[20] We have already noted[21] that Marxism, according to Mao, considers the struggle of opposites as absolute. Freud too was led by his study of man to believe that the irrational is more fundamental than the rational.

Of course, the theory of evolution, as it was understood in the nineteenth century, gave a tremendous fillip to this point of view. Nature was conceived in terms of the struggle for existence, 'red in tooth and claw'. The great philosopher of evolution, Friedrich Nietzsche, despised the Christian virtues of meekness and humility, or rather denied that they are virtues at all. He saw them as hindrances in the way of the evolution of the superman, who can realize himself only through struggle. 'Doth not man's *future* strive and thrust in you?' he asks: 'Man's furthest, deepest, starhighest essence, his prodigious power – do not all these seethe together in your vessels?' And since this will to power is primary, it is not surprising that Nietzsche also writes: 'You shall love peace as a means to new wars – and short peace rather than long! Let your peace be victory!'[22]

But in the history of philosophy we find a contrasting view, one that is closer to the biblical thinking about these matters, for it holds peace and rationality to be primary. This view too has had its distinguished advocates. In English philosophy, one may mention especially Richard Hooker, John Locke and Joseph Butler. We might call this the 'natural law' tradition, for it believes that even in the so-called 'state of nature' some actions are already just and others unjust, for there is a law given with human nature itself, prior to any conventions or to any positive law, and indeed shaping these. We can let John Locke be the spokesman for this point of view, since he offers an interesting contrast to Thomas Hobbes. The state of nature and the state of war are not the same. They are 'as far distant as a state of peace, goodwill, mutual assistance and preservation and a state of enmity, malice, violence and mutual destruction are from one another'. The state of nature is 'men living together according to reason'. Or, as he also says, 'the state of nature has a law of nature to govern it, which obliges everyone, and reason, which is that law, teaches all mankind who will but consult it, that being all equal and independent, no one ought to harm another in his life, health, liberty or possessions'.[23] This view expressed by Locke is in the sharpest opposition to the view exemplified by Hobbes. Incidentally, if the view of Hobbes derived some support from the nine-teenth-century understanding of evolution as a gigantic strug-gle for survival, it may be that the view of Locke is closer to twentieth-century understandings of evolution, for many bio-logists have been stressing the importance of co-operation and symbiosis in evolutionary advance, and nature as a whole has been portrayed as an intricate eco-system based on interdepen-dence rather than as the theatre of uncontrolled competition.

But how does one decide between the two views before us? Is peace the primary human condition and war a falling away? Or is struggle the final reality? Or are the two perhaps equally matched?

Before we attempt to answer the question, we must note a peculiarity which attaches to it, as indeed to all questions about the nature of man. The very answer that we give will to some extent shape the human reality itself. When we discuss man, we are not describing an indifferent reality. We are trying to reach a self-understanding, and the way we under-stand ourselves helps to make us who we are and influences the way we behave. If, for instance, it is our conviction that strug-gle is the fundamental reality, then it would make sense to go on from there to adopt the political dictum of Machiavelli that a ruler 'should have no other aim or thought, nor take up any other thing for his study, but war and its organization and dis-cipline'.[24]

There is much in the history of human society and in its pre-sent condition that would seem to support this opinion. Is it not just common-sense realism to acknowledge that men are fundamentally aggressive and competitive, that our policies should be framed with this fact in view, and that peace can be at most a palliative? Yet if one can point to many evidences to show that war is the natural human condition, there are other evidences that count on the opposite side. For instance, anthro-pologists, explorers and missionaries sometimes come across tribes that live peaceably and are unacquainted with the arts of war.[25] Again, even where war is common, the relations of tribes and nations have from the earliest times been subject to some elementary rules of justice and humanity, sometimes called the *jus gentium* or law of nations, a kind of natural law on an international scale. The inviolability of ambassadors, the obligation to respect a truce, the right of prisoners to humane treatment – these have been almost universally recognized as binding norms of political behaviour, and even if men have often failed to observe these norms, such failures have been reprobated as barbarous and inhuman acts. The very sense of outrage provoked by such conduct is itself significant. This significance is well expressed by Reinhold Niebuhr: 'The disorder of war would not be an evil did it not operate within and against some kind of harmony and interdependence of nations.'[26]

I believe that interdependence and harmony are more ultimate than the disorder of war, but it must be confessed that it is an ambiguous picture that confronts us. In the socio-political life of man we see both rationality and irrationality, both aggression and co-operation, both antipathy and sympathy. There is no finally conclusive empirical evidence that can demonstrate the primacy *as a matter of fact* of peace over war or of war over peace.

But this is not merely a question of fact, or merely an empirical question, though empirical considerations are not irrelevant. For questions relating to man always carry us beyond the describable facts of his existence. Human nature is not a fixed essence, given as something ready made, and then to be described by observation. Human nature is still emerging, and its future shape and ultimate goals are not yet fully determined. Though they will be partly determined by forces that operate outside of man, they will also be partly determined by his own decisions and evaluations, and not least by the beliefs that he holds about himself. It would be impossible to prove that the biblical notion of peace as *shalom* has an objective truth that is denied to the notion of peace as *pax*; or that Locke's view of man as by nature rational and sociable has, as a factual description, more evidence to support it than Hobbes' view that the state of nature is a state of war. But even to hold one or other of these views tends to bring about the state of affairs which it envisages. In each case the first alternative promotes an attitude of trust which prevents the breakdown of communication and the widening of alienation, and so conduces to an affirmative relationship; while the second alternative undermines trust and fosters fear and alienation. In questions like these, a decision must be *to some extent* a decision of faith, though assuredly a decision that remains in touch with the empirical facts, so far as these are discernible.

Is it worthwhile then to accept the biblical conception of peace and the understanding of human nature implied in it? It cannot be objectively proved, and to accept it is to take a risk. Yet only some such conception seems to hold out an ultimate hope for mankind. At least, we can agree that there is something here worthy of further exploration.

NOTES

1. Francis Brown, S.R. Driver and C.A. Briggs, *Hebrew and English Lexicon of the Old Testament*, Oxford University Press 1907, p.1022.
2. Werner Foerster in *Theological Dictionary of the New Testament*, ed. G. Kittel, tr. G.W. Bromiley, Eerdmans 1964, vol. II, pp.401f.
3. *Quotations from Chairman Mao Tse-Tung*, Foreign Languages Press, Peking 1966, p.214.
4. See below, pp.22ff.
5. Isa. 2.2-4.
6. Isa. 9.6.
7. C.F. Evans in *A Theological Wordbook of the Bible*, ed. Alan Richardson, SCM Press 1957, p.165.
8. Zech. 8.12.

9. Ezek. 34.25.

10. Isa. 35.1.

11. Isa 11.6-9.

12. Isa. 48.22.

13. John 14.27.

14. Eph. 2.14.

15. Eph. 2.14f.

16. Eph. 2.13.

17. Col. 1.24.

18. Matt. 5.9.

19. Thomas Hobbes, *Leviathan*, ed. M. Oakeshott, Blackwell 1934, pp.80ff.

20. Carl von Clausewitz, *On War*, tr. J.J. Graham, Penguin 1968, p.402.

21. See above, p.16.

22. Friedrich Nietzsche, *Thus Spake Zarathustra*, tr. A. Tille and M.M. Bozman, Dent 1933, pp.39,258.

23. John Locke, *Of Civil Government*, Dent 1924, pp.119,126.

24. Niccolo Machiavelli, *The Prince*, tr. L. Ricci, Oxford University Press 1903, p.65.

25. Cf. the Abbé Dubois on some of the inhabitants of southern India as he found them at the end of the eighteenth century: 'All these wild tribes are gentle and peaceable by nature. They do not understand the use of weapons of any sort . . . they do not know what war means' (*Hindu Manners, Customs and Ceremonies*, Oxford University Press 1906, p.79).

26. Reinhold Niebuhr, *The Nature and Destiny of Man*, Nisbet 1941–3, vol. I, p.282.

THREE

Dynamics of Peace

In the last chapter two contrasting views of peace were delineated. On the one view, peace was conceived in an affirmative way, with conflict secondary; this is the view which we have found in the biblical teaching, as well as in some other traditions, both philosophical and pre-philosophical. On the other view, conflict is the natural human condition, with peace secondary; and we have seen that this view is also represented at both the philosophical and pre-philosophical levels. The question arises whether that first view is not too idealistic and utopian to be of any practical value. The other view seems to be far more realistic and to have a far more obvious bearing on those actual problems which at the present day seem to offer a threat to peace.

But this very expression, 'threat to peace', is a thoroughly question-begging phrase. It assumes that there already is in existence a state of affairs worthy to be called 'peace', and this is exactly what those who take an affirmative view of peace might be disposed to deny. Going back to the biblical tradition, we find that the Hebrew prophets had little patience with a so-called peace which meant simply the absence of overt conflict, for that peace fell far short of what they understood by the fullness of *shalom*, and might even be destructive of a true *shalom*. Looking round Israel, Jeremiah saw indeed a nation that was for the time being free from open violence.

But it was a nation without integrity, for, as he put it, 'from the greatest to the least of them, everyone is greedy for unjust gain'. And in the face of that situation, he declared: 'They have healed the wound of my people lightly, saying, "Peace, peace", when there is no peace.'[1] One may compare with this the remark which Tacitus attributes to a British chieftain concerning the invading Roman legions: 'They have made a desolation, and they call it peace.' This is one possible view of the *pax Romana*. If we understand peace affirmatively as wholeness rather than negatively as the absence of war, then in some circumstances the gravest threat to peace might come not from those who were trying to stir up some conflict but from those who supinely acquiesced in the existing state of affairs. Conversely, a man like Jeremiah can be seen not as a troubler of the peace but as one dedicated to a peace that is more than superficial.

The relation between peace and conflict is a very complex one, and we shall have to explore it rather carefully if we are not to fall into oversimplified positions. It is this relation which sets up what I call the dynamics of peace. Yet before we consider this question further, let me concede that even if one holds an affirmative view of peace, nevertheless at any given time the proximate task may be the negative one of preventing an unacceptable level of conflict. The affirmative concept of peace, as we have claimed, is not merely an eschatological vision but a constant pressure on the day-to-day decisions of those who entertain it. Frequently the only possibility open may be the very humble and unexciting one of reducing hostility and violence.

There are interesting illustrations of this in the history of the Christian understanding of peace. In the rough feudal times of the Middle Ages, violence and bloodshed were commonplace. In the tenth century the church authorities in France began to develop the idea of a 'peace of God'. It sought to exempt certain persons from violence and to ban fighting on Sundays. The so-called 'truce of God' went even further. It forbade fighting from Saturday night until Monday morning, and the ban came to be extended to other holy days and seasons. Historian Latourette remarks: 'Never fully enforced, it exercised some restraint on the disorders of the time.'[2] The church also discouraged jousting, since this was both an incentive to violence and a source of feuding.

Yet the strange contradictions in human nature and the way in which our aggressive and peace-loving instincts seem to be intertwined is afforded by the action of the Council of Clermont in 1095. On the one hand, this Council endorsed the peace of God and tried to spread it throughout Christendom. On the other hand, the same Council launched the First Crusade, so plunging Europe into many decades of fruitless violence.

Nevertheless, I mention these modest attempts to restrain the worse forms of violence to show that the Christian eschatological vision of peace is not merely utopian and does not prevent engagement with the immediate issues. In our own time also, the most pressing issues of peace are concerned with the negative task of avoiding or reducing violent confrontations. Disarmament, for instance, may be only a first step towards peace in the full sense, but it is a very important one, for the more arms proliferate, the more danger there is of armed conflict. This applies not only between states but within any society. One can 'feel' the difference and the relaxation of tension as one moves from a country where firearms are common and where the police find it necessary to carry firearms, as in the United States, to a country where firearms are not common and where the police do not normally carry them, as in England. Another illustration of the urgency of the negative task of simply reducing frictions is afforded by the existence at any given time of a number of situations of severe strain around the world. These are, so to speak, flashpoints where explosions have become imminent. Relations have been strained to the point at which communication ceases and open hostility breaks out. The immediate task of peace may be simply to ease the situation at one of these danger points.

Yet all this is far from showing that the affirmative vision of peace as *shalom* is merely a utopian dream and has no relevance to the nicely calculated more or less of actual situations where one is confronted with the reality of conflict and the clash of seemingly irreconcileable interests. On the contrary, there might be little justification for disarming or reducing tension unless one could look beyond the immediate reduction of the level of conflict to an affirmative goal in which the deep-lying causes of the conflict are resolved in a just manner. If some such affirmative understanding of peace is not present, then there is no answer to those who say that so far from reducing friction, it should be our business to increase the friction and carry through the conflict to the point of resolution, even violent resolution. For we come back to the point that for many people in the world today, the word 'peace' must have as cynical a ring as it did for the British chieftain who saw the *pax Romana* as desolation. For 'peace' is too often understood as simply the damping down of conflicts which were aiming at changing the *status quo*.

Let us accept that an eschatological ideal of peace, expressed perhaps in theological or metaphysical terms, is, when taken in isolation, remote from our actual situations and to that extent irrelevant. But let us not suppose that one becomes realistic and practical by confining attention to the actual conflicts and aggressions that are going on among men at any given moment, as if these were the primary reality. The understanding of peace which we have met in Christianity and in the natural law type of political philosophy is essentially a correct and realistic one. But in view of our discussions, it now has to be stated more clearly that in the Christian concept of peace, although wholeness is held to be more primordial than conflict, the fact of conflict is not denied. However, conflict is included within wholeness and is made to subserve it. This means that the Christian concept of peace is a thoroughly dynamic one. It can have nothing to do with a mere tranquillizing of the world, with the elimination of war and the holding down of levels of conflict without regard to the state of affairs that is being preserved in this way. If peace is indeed finally wholeness, then there can be no rest until the possibility of wholeness and fulfilment has been opened up for all men; and obviously there will have to be a lot of conflict of one kind or another before that can happen. Peace is dynamic in the sense that although its foundation is that wholeness which is proper to human nature, this very wholeness must take up conflict and difference. Peace is therefore a striving. Those who advocate peace in a world where there is so much deprivation and oppression can only hope to do so successfully if they can demonstrate that their understanding of peace is thoroughly dynamic. They must expound a concept of peace that will be seen as a growing edge into a changing and better order, and demonstrate that this dynamic way of peace is better than the way of violence.

This teaching about peace is, of course, plainly set forth in the New Testament. The words of Christ about leaving the gift of peace to his disciples, quoted in an earlier chapter,[3] occur in the context of those discourses in which he warns his disciples about their coming conflict with the commonly accepted standards of the world. Elsewhere in the New Testament, Christ says: 'I came not to send peace, but a sword', and he visualizes that his teaching and mission will deeply divide men.[4] This may seem to be in contradiction to what we have been saying earlier about the inclusive virtue of peace bringing wholeness to every area of life and overcoming division and alienation. But it is not contradictory; it is an expression of the dynamic character of any peace that is worthy to be called peace. Dom Helder Camara, bishop of an underdeveloped area of Brazil, writes in a book with the significant title *Revolution through Peace*: 'There is no doubt that Christ came to bring peace to men. But not the peace of stagnant swamps, not peace based on injustice, not peace that is the opposite of development. In such cases Christ himself proclaimed that he had come to bring strife and a sword.'[5]

I have consistently maintained that peace is more primordial than war in the human condition, yet this affirmation has to be understood in such a way that it recognizes also the reality of conflict, even the necessity and value of conflict. I have in fact also urged that conflict can be creative.[6] But conflict must be included within wholeness. A wholeness which did not include conflict would be a frozen condition, a kind of death lacking dynamism and the possibility of new development. On the other hand, conflict that has broken away from the goal of wholeness has become quite negative and destructive, and can no longer serve the cause of a more fulfilled humanity.

Here we may recall that third pre-philosophical way of conceiving peace which was mentioned in connection with the Chinese conception of peace as the harmonization or tension of opposites.[7] The advantage of such a conception is that it stresses the dynamic character of peace. This is conceived neither as an end state of absolute rest nor as a temporary pause in the violence of conflict, but more as a state of equilibrium in which powerful forces are thrusting, though in such a way that a wholeness is maintained and there is no blind clash of opposites. Perhaps the analogy of a biological organism is a good illustration.

A modern writer who has developed in some detail the notion of peace as dynamic equilibrium is Eugen Rosenstock-

Huessy.[8] Any society, as he sees it, can be regarded as existing on two axes, a temporal axis and spatial axis. Along these axes, it is subject to the strain of opposing forces which encounter the society on four fronts — the past and the future, the outside and the inside. Peace is the condition in which the society can survive and develop through the interaction of these forces, without being torn apart by them. Peace becomes the art, based on social experience and social knowledge, of maintaining a balance between the claims of the past and those of the future, so that the society is neither submerged in traditionalism and decadence nor plunged into uncontrolled revolutionary change; and likewise, of so balancing the outward thrust of the society with its inward structures that it neither makes aggressive war upon its neighbours nor collapses in anarchy upon itself.

This is an ingenious theory with possibilities for development to which my bare summary does little justice. But it is liable to one misunderstanding. It might be supposed that even if this way of conceiving peace does introduce a definitely dynamic element and gets away from the thought of peace as merely rest, it is finally not dynamic enough, for the notion of an equilibrium seems to visualize no change in the total situation, whatever adjustments and interactions may be taking place within it. This, I think, is a misunderstanding, for we find Rosenstock-Huessy talking in ways which do indicate that his idea of peace is wedded to that of change. He points out, of course, that change itself is ambiguous, and there is no virtue in change for change's sake. But he goes on to say: 'Peace is the experience of change at the right time. The best change is a peaceful change. Peace is not a situation that obstructs change or history or reform. Peace presupposes change and time processes.'[9]

Why then can Rosenstock-Huessy's theory be so easily misunderstood? The answer, I think, is the inadequacy of his model, that of the equilibrium of forces. Although I have said that this model and its Chinese prototype have the advantage of stressing the dynamic character of peace, I believe that finally the biblical model is more adequate, provided that its eschatological ideal of wholeness is always seen to include the process of conflict and differentiation by which alone the wholeness of persons in community can be reached. Indeed, one might argue that the three pre-philosophical concepts of peace which I distinguished in an earlier chapter[10] correspond to three pre-philosophical conceptions of history, and that the notion of peace is in each case appropriate to a particular notion of history. The classical understanding of peace as the truce or interval between recurrent outbreaks of the fundamental war or *polemos* fits in well with the cyclic understanding of history, also current in classical thought, the view that everything reverts to its former condition. The Chinese understanding of peace as the harmony of opposites accords with the Chinese view of history as the rhythmic ebb and flow of the cosmic principles in a pattern which Toynbee[11] has compared to the musical form of a theme and variations and which, he suggests, combines something of the classical cyclic view of history with features which are more clearly visible in the biblical view. This biblical view of history is itself conceived on the linear model; history has a beginning and it moves towards an end or *eschaton*, and perhaps it is only some such view of history as this that allows for the emergence of the really new. But this historical movement towards the fulfilment of eschatological peace proceeds by way of struggle – the shattering and remaking of Israel in the Old Testament, the death and resurrection of Christ in the New. Peace as the wholeness of *shalom* is the end and goal of history, but it includes the process by which it is to be attained, that is to say, it includes strife, struggle, suffering, and is dynamic in the highest degree.

To make such statements, however, is to be brought to the

edge of some very difficult and controversial questions. No one perhaps is going to quarrel with the belief that biblical and Christian teaching point us to peace as the goal of human existence. But we are now saying that they likewise teach the necessity and perhaps even the duty of conflict on the way to attaining that goal. What kind of conflict might be encouraged? Does Christianity condone violence as a means towards the end of peace? And if so, under what circumstances and to what extent would the end be taken to justify the means? Such questions cannot be avoided if we are willing to take in earnest the biblical understanding that any peace worthy of the name can never be simply the preservation of tranquillity but must be a peace based on justice and offering the possibility of fulfilment to all. But it is not easy to answer these questions, and there is sharp division among Christians themselves as to how they should be answered.

Does Christianity condone violence? Perhaps the first point to be made in answer to this question is just to point out that in fact Christianity has again and again condoned violence in the course of its history. Catholic popes and bishops have marched at the head of armies, Protestant reformers have led revolts and tyrannized over cities, churchmen of all sorts have entreated God to grant victory to the armies of their respective nations. Whether any of them ought to have done these things is, of course, another question. But that Christians have believed it their duty to support violent action or even to engage in it themselves is nothing new. Thus if someone today urges, for example, that Christians should support some violent group that is rebelling against an oppressive regime, there is not much point in expressing shock or pained surprise over the claim. It is very much in line with a long history of Christian support for violence. But it does remain to ask whether such an attitude, either now or in the past, can be held to be morally and theologically justifiable or even politically expedient.

Discussion of these matters is often confused by the use of terms that have been inadequately defined or are even tendentious. So before we go on to the difficult questions of peace and violence, it will be well worth our while to pause and make a few distinctions and clarifications.

Let us begin with the notion of power. By 'power' is meant the capacity to initiate action and to bring about change. Power is exercised both by individuals and by groups, and it is of many kinds – military power, economic power, political power and so on. There cannot be truly human persons or truly human communities without power, for if there is no power, then there is no freedom to act, and the freedom to act is a basic constituent of human and personal being. If people, whether individuals or groups, are deprived of power, then they are also being deprived of the capacity for a fully human mode of existence. They are being depressed below the level of such an existence.

Now if peace as *shalom* means wholeness or fullness of existence for all, then it follows that this state of affairs cannot be attained until all have a share in the power which is an essential ingredient in a fully human existence. Hence, a dynamic concept of peace envisages a distribution of power. The concentration of power may lead to a seeming peace, an outward tranquillity of the *pax Romana* type; but there can be peace in the affirmative sense only as power concentrations are broken up and more and more people have a share in the power of deciding about their own future and the future of our planet. To exercise power and to know freedom belong to the essence of human individuals and human communities.

But immediately we strike a difficulty that makes any easy solution impossible. The desire for power and freedom of action is natural to the human being. Indeed, he cannot be human without it. But because human existence is distorted, the will to power can become a great evil, for people and groups are not content with a just share of power. They seek an excess of power and they seek to rob others of power, or to keep them deprived of power. Thus there inevitably arises a power struggle, and in that struggle it is very rare (I would not say that it never happens) for a group to give up voluntarily some of its power. In any case, it has been argued on the other side, notably by Franz Fanon, that the powerless groups can only attain the dignity of freedom if they *seize* power for themselves. It is not something that can be given, it must be taken. I think myself that Fanon makes the serious mistake of confusing power with violence, but of this I shall say more later.

But to come back to the argument, we see going on a struggle for the fairer distribution of power, and this is a necessary stage on the way to peace in the full sense. And we must notice also that no one and no group can be truly at peace until there is the general enjoyment of power and freedom. Aristotle's doctrine of the mean in ethics has much wisdom in it. If some men and groups are dehumanized through power-lessness and lack of freedom, others are dehumanized through an excess of power. Hegel's famous analysis of the master-slave relationship[12] made it plain that both suffer and both need to be set free. As black theologian James Cone has put it, 'No man is free until all men are free.'[13] We could equally well say that no man has peace until all men enjoy peace.

Let us be careful too not to oversimplify by putting all the blame on one side, for there is no monopoly of sin in human affairs. No doubt a special responsibility lies with those in whose hands are the reins of power. Yet it is also true, as Reinhold Niebuhr has remarked, that 'every victim of injustice makes the mistake of supposing that the sin from which he suffers is a peculiar vice of his oppressor. This is the self-righteousness of the weak as distinct from the self-righteousness of the powerful.'[14] There will be no advance towards peace until all groups have put away their self-righteousness.

Our discussion of power brought us to the power struggle, so next we turn to the notion of conflict. Like power, conflict is of many things, and again like power, it seems to be essential to the human condition. Conflict occurs when individuals or groups or even ideas with contradictory claims come into confrontation with each other. I have stressed several times that conflict is not in itself a bad thing. I doubt if there could be persons of any depth if they had not experienced conflict. Man's character and skills have been strengthened through his conflict with nature; the conflict of the sexes and the generations has been enriching for society, as has also been the conflict of cultures; truth in the intellectual disciplines can be gained only through the conflict of rival ideas. But just as power is ambiguous, so that excessive power dehumanizes, so is conflict ambiguous. Conflicts must not be resolved too quickly. They must be brought into the open and even on occasion intensified, or otherwise they may be simply swept under the carpet to breed on there and to erupt in a worse form later. Yet once again it is necessary to have the wisdom to recognize the mean. Conflicts continue to have the possibility of being creative so long as there remains some communication, some reciprocity, between the conflicting parties. Conflicts in this sense (and quite sharp ones) must be faced and even sometimes provoked if there is to be any advance toward a true peace, which is a peace dynamically conceived.

But the tragedy is that conflict so easily gets out of hand. Communication and reciprocity cease. The creative possibilities are swallowed up by the destructive tendencies. The danger now is not that the conflict will be resolved too quickly, but that it never will be resolved at all. For it has been decided to coerce the other side, and coercion in itself will not get to the root of the difference.

There are different modes of coercion and different degrees of pressure brought to bear on the other side. Some distinctions are worth making, though in practice it may be difficult to maintain them, and one form tends to pass over into another. Nevertheless, there are forms of non-violent coercion – strikes, boycotts, demonstrations and the like within a community, economic sanctions in international relations, and so on. Again, any state has to use force for the restraint of its anti-social members, but if this force is held down to minimal levels, we would not normally call it violence. The term 'violence' is properly used when the restraints that govern non-violent action or the legitimate use of force are set aside and all means, including the infliction of death and injury, are used for the subjection of the other side. War is the most massive and excessive of all forms of violence.

The disorder of war and violence, whether it takes place between sovereign states or within a state that is torn by civil strife, is something that no one in his senses could desire if he could find any other way of handling the conflict. But in fact wars and violence do occur, and there is no sign that they are going away in the contemporary world. They are still advocated by some as necessary evils and even as necessary means on the way to eventual peace. Can this ever be so? The question will be pursued in the next chapter.

NOTES

1. Jer. 6.13f.
2. K.S. Latourette, *A History of Christianity*, Eyre and Spottiswoode 1953, p.475.
3. See above, p.20.
4. Matt.10.34.
5. Helder Camara, *Revolution through Peace*, tr. A. McLean, Harper and Row 1971, p.130.
6. See above, p.30.

7. See above, p.16.

8. In *Speech and Reality*, Argo Books 1970, and other writings.

9. Op. cit., p.35.

10. See above, pp.14ff.

11. A. J. Toynbee, *An Historian's Approach to Religion*, Oxford University Press 1956, p.12.

12. G.W.F. Hegel, *The Phenomenology of Mind*, tr. J.B. Baillie, Allen and Unwin 1931, pp.228ff.

13. James H. Cone, *A Black Theology of Liberation*, Lippincott 1970, p.160.

14. Reinhold Niebuhr, *The Nature and Destiny of Man*, Nisbet 1941-3, vol. I, p.240.

FOUR

Peace and Violence

War, we have noted, is the most massive form of violence. It is also the least restrained, for although some conventions are accepted even in war, these tend to become eroded away as the struggle becomes more intensified.

In our time feelings about war have become very ambivalent. On the one hand, the bitter experience of two quite unprecedented world wars in the twentieth century has led to a revulsion of feeling against war, a revulsion which is likewise quite unprecedented in its scope and intensity. It may simply be the case, of course, that the prospect of a third world war is so frightening because of the destruction and suffering that such a war would cause that war on this scale has now become unthinkable as an instrument of policy. It cannot be denied that terror has been an extremely efficient deterrent from total war ever since the first atomic bomb was used at Hiroshima. Yet I venture to think there is more to it than that. There seems to have been a definite shift of values in recent times. At least in the older and more mature nations, the patriotic and martial virtues, once so highly esteemed, have been losing ground. They no longer turn people on, so to speak, in the way that they once did. The high valuation placed on these virtues in the past is now openly questioned.

This may be a hopeful sign. It is to be seen as part of a more general revulsion against the accepted values of Western society. This is the revulsion which has produced the phenomenon sometimes known as the counter-culture. This has many features, but typically it is directed not only against the values of an aggressive society but equally against the values of an acquisitive society. It sees these two sets of values as intimately intertwined and supporting one another in the so-called 'military-industrial' complex.

On the other hand, one must acknowledge that there always have been ambivalent feelings on these matters. There have always been peaceable individuals as well as warlike ones, doves as well as hawks. And likewise, it would seem, there have always been peace-loving nations and tribes alongside others whose tempers have been aggressive and who have enlarged themselves through despoiling their industrious neighbours.

But over and above any gain that war and violence might bring, there is a subtler attractiveness about them. It is not hard to see some of the elements of this attractiveness. War challenges men by calling forth special skills as they pit their wits against the enemy for the highest stakes. War does engender courage and self-sacrifice and a quite unique kind of comradeship among those who share in the ups and downs of a campaign. War does provide an excitement that can give life a new interest for those whose ordinary existence has been dull and mechanical. In one of James Jones' novels, two veterans of World War II are spending a vacation in the West Indies. They fall to discussing their histories, and come to the conclusion that nothing interesting has happened to either of them since the end of the war.

An incident like that makes one wonder whether we have reckoned sufficiently with the fact of boredom in the contemporary world, and what boredom does to people. Both risk and variety have been greatly diminished by the spread all over the world of a uniform technological civilization. Travel, for instance, has become so cheap, so swift, so painless, that it has lost much of its charm and excitement. We are sated with it. Sport has become so commercialized and politicized that it too becomes a bore.

According to Milton, 'Peace hath her victories, no less renowned than war', but it must frankly be admitted that it is difficult to make the tasks of peace as exciting as those of war. Indeed, as we all know, many of the important medical and technical discoveries of recent times were made under the pressure of war, and only subsequently applied for peaceful purposes. Roger Shinn raises a very searching critical question when he writes: 'If we ask why modern society is so sterile in enabling people to find in peace a gratification that is common in war, we may have begun a profound interrogation of our culture.'[1]

He himself no doubt gives part of the answer when he writes elsewhere in his book: 'Peace may be a rationalization of the comfort and irresponsibility of the uncommitted.'[2] That, of course, would be only a false peace, for we have seen that any true peace includes dynamism and conflict. My insistence on this element of conflict in peace now obtains an additional vindication, for if peace is to claim the enthusiasm and spur the imaginations of men as wars have done in the past, then it must be as exciting as war and give scope for the skills and emotional experiences that war called forth. But how is this to happen? Does the need to include conflict in peace mean that violence itself is to be employed or harnessed in the pursuit of peace? Is the violence that once expressed itself in wars among the nations now to find expression in revolutionary activities aimed at the violent overthrow of existing institutions but with the ultimate goal of establishing a true *shalom* for those who are at present deprived?

And here we strike on another aspect of the ambiguity of the present situation. On the one hand there has been, as I have said, a revulsion of feeling against large-scale international war, and the threat of a third world war seems to have receded somewhat. But there is no evidence that war and violence are going away. They are very much with us, but in other forms. Very costly and bloody local wars keep breaking out on different parts of the earth's surface, and some of them drag on for years. Some of them greatly exceed in destructiveness quite major wars of earlier centuries.

But the most typical form of warfare that has emerged in our time is the so-called 'guerrilla' war. A new kind of violence has become widespread, so that hardly any country is now free from it. We have all become familiar with the techniques of this new kind of violence. Skyjackings, kidnappings, bombing of public places, sniping, intimidation, assassinations – these have become everyday occurrences in the world of the late twentieth century. Furthermore, it has become clear that in our tightly knit world, a very small group of really ruthless and determined people can so disrupt the life of society that their demands cannot be ignored. And there are some evidences that only when deprived groups engage in this kind of violent activity does society begin to listen to their grievances and take steps to remedy them. In some cases where oppression and neglect had gone on for years – and such oppression and neglect, it is sometimes argued, is itself a covert form of violence, a systemic violence built into the social and political structures – in some such cases, a single violent outburst of rioting by the victims has been enough to jolt the authorities out of their complacency.

But whether any genuine solutions are to be found along these lines is a different question, and one to which we shall pay attention shortly. For the present, it may be enough to point out that one of the most obvious and most reprehensible features of the new violence is its completely indiscriminate character. The acts which are typical of it, such as taking hostages, bombing public places or public transport and the like, are directed against everybody in general and nobody in particular. Many of the victims of this kind of violence have been innocent people, not directly concerned in the quarrel. In all wars, of course, there have been incidental and accidental victims. But it is evidence of a new spirit of ruthlessness when violence is directed indiscriminately against the community at large. Thus however much one might sympathize with the plight of groups who in their frustration turn to such violence, I do not think that finally one can condone it. I do not believe either that such violence can in the long run be productive of good results. It is more likely to be counter-productive and to work against the interests of the very people whom it is supposed to serve.

But it is a further evidence of the moral ambiguity of our current situation that many of the very people who have turned away in horror and revulsion from conventional war seem to have a measure of sympathy with the new kind of violence that I have been describing. There is even an attempt to throw a certain romantic glamour over revolutionary fighters against oppressive or supposedly oppressive regimes in different parts of the world. Some Christians too have come to believe that it is right for them to give support, moral and financial, to groups engaging in violent revolutionary activity.

And here we must notice that ambivalent feelings about violence seem to afflict Christians just as much as other people. There is no clear universally accepted Christian teaching on the subject. There has been on the one hand a long Christian tradition of pacifism and non-violence, but alongside it there has been another tradition, not, indeed, encouraging violence, yet deeming it to be permissible and even necessary in certain circumstances.

At first sight, the teaching and example of Jesus himself seems to afford considerable support for those who believe that Christianity commits one to non-violent means of effecting change. The Sermon on the Mount deplores the spirit of retaliation. 'Do not resist one who is evil,' teaches Jesus, 'but if any one strikes you on the right cheek, turn to him the other also; and if any one would sue you and take your coat, let him have your cloak as well; and if any one forces you to go one mile, go with him two miles.' Again, he bids his followers: 'Love your enemies and pray for those who persecute you.'[3] This is not only a doctrine of non-violence; it would seem to be a doctrine of non-resistance. Or rather, it is the doctrine that evil cannot be resisted by a further evil, but rather by a good which is willing to absorb the outrage of the evil and by absorbing it to overcome it. Jesus' teaching is taken up by his followers. 'Do not be overcome by evil,' writes Paul, 'but overcome evil with good.'[4]

But it is not simply the teaching of Jesus and his followers that makes the point. Jesus' own career is depicted in the gospels as that of a suffering Messiah. He gives himself up to death for the sake of effecting an atonement that will overcome the alienation that separates men from one another and from God. And if, as Christians believe, God himself is revealed in Jesus Christ, then this God is not an arbitrary monarch disposing events with unlimited power, but a God who in Christ places himself at the disposal of violent men and shares in the suffering of his creatures. Theologian Gordon Kaufman goes so far as to claim that non-resistance is one of the basic attributes of God. 'The Christian gospel,' he maintains, 'is no announcement that God enters into community with men and overcomes their rebellion through *compelling* obedience against their will. Quite the contrary. It is through suffering the cross which men inflict on him that he wins over their hearts in spite of themselves.'[5] Kaufman goes on to quote the well-known words of Bonhoeffer, to the effect that 'God lets himself be pushed out of the world on to the cross. He is weak and powerless in the world, and that is precisely the way, the only way, in which he is with us and helps us.'[6]

During its early history, the church continued to follow the paths of non-resistance and non-violence. Admittedly, its motives differed in some ways from those of modern pacifists. The early Christians were above all concerned not to be involved in paganism, so that in many matters they constituted a group that was alienated from the mainstream of society. Thus Christians did not serve in the imperial armies. They stayed away from the public entertainments involving violence and bloodshed, except indeed when they were taken there as the victims. But it was through acceptance of their sufferings that the Christians finally overcame the persecution of the authorities. The blood of the martyrs proved indeed to be the seed of the church.

But after the emperor Constantine had established his position by force of arms and had brought to an end the persecution of the church, Christian attitudes began to change. In the new situation we find St Augustine, for instance, writing to a young man: 'Do not think that it is impossible for anyone to please God while engaged in active military service.'[7] Yet it would be wrong to conclude cynically that the change in the church's situation was the sole cause that led to the abandonment of pacifist attitudes. An ambiguity had been there from the beginning. For while the New Testament has its teaching on non-resistance, it also has quite definite teaching on the Christian's duty to the state.[8] Christianity did not mean dropping out of the world, but living in a tension or dialectic with the world. And it is impossible to do this without in some ways participating in the corporate sins of the world, including its violence.

Christians today are still divided on the question of whether their faith commits them to refrain from any forms of war and violence, and one finds sincere and able men taking different sides on this issue. The problem is well illustrated by the case of Bonhoeffer. I mentioned a moment ago his teaching about God's non-resistance, God's weakness and powerlessness in the world. Yet this same Bonhoeffer believed it was his duty to engage in a conspiracy which plotted the violent overthrow of the Hitler régime in Germany.

The rise of the Nazis in Germany was in fact an event which raised very serious questions for pacifism. Many who belonged to the generation which grew up after the First World War, myself among them, were ardent pacifists. We believed that non-violence offered the only way to a just and peaceful world order. But the mounting aggressions of the Nazis, culminating in the outbreak of war in 1939, led many of us to the conviction that the strictly pacifist position is too simple and that sometimes there is a duty to participate even in the violence of war. Bertrand Russell in his *Autobiography* refers to the change that came over his beliefs at that time, and his experience was a common one. He writes: 'I had allowed a larger sphere to the method of non-resistance – or, rather, non-violent resistance – than later experience seemed to warrant. It certainly has an important sphere; as against the British in India, Gandhi led it to triumph. But it depends upon the existence of certain virtues in those against whom it is employed. When Indians lay down on railways and challenged the authorities to crush them under trains, the British found such cruelty intolerable. But the Nazis had no scruples in analogous situations.'[9] It should be noted that it is not being said that non-violent methods should be abandoned. They can be effective in certain circumstances, that is to say, when dealing with authorities which have what I would call a 'natural law' mentality. Russell mentions Gandhi's use of non-violent methods against British rule in India, and one might add as another illustration Martin Luther King's use of similar methods in the United States. But if one were dealing with a completely ruthless enemy who rejected any restraint arising from the acknowledgement of a natural law, then it might be argued that one is thrown back on violence. This is certainly how many people did feel in the face of Hitler's Germany, and Stalin's Russia might be cited as another instance of quite ruthless force. Even so, however, we have to recall that the persecuting might of the Roman Empire, sometimes unleashed with great severity, was not able to crush the Christian church and in the end was overcome by it.

In any case, it is very easy for reactions to become exaggerated, so that people pass from one extreme to another. The total commitment to non-resistance or at least to non-violent resistance which was widespread among Christians of a generation ago but which was seen to be an oversimplified attitude when the Nazis rose to power has been succeeded nowadays by a tendency even among Christians to accept violence too quickly and too lightly. The picture of Jesus as the preacher and practitioner of non-resistance has been replaced by a new picture of Jesus as a violent revolutionary. Actually, this is not in the least a new picture, for though it has figured prominently in some recent literature, this was the picture which was presented by one of the pioneers of modern biblical criticism, the eighteenth-century scholar Samuel Reimarus.[10] He believed that when Jesus proclaimed the advent of the kingdom of God, that could be understood by the people in only one sense, namely, the political sense. Jesus was proclaiming liberation from the domination of the Romans. His triumphal entry into Jerusalem and his violent expulsion of the money-changers and merchants from the Temple are seen by Reimarus as his attempt to start an insurrection. But it seems that Jesus had overestimated the extent of his support among the populace. His followers melted away, he found himself isolated, arrested, condemned. His political mission had been a failure. And the cry of dereliction from the cross, 'My God, my God, why hast thou forsaken me?', is his own acknowledgment of that failure.

This, in summary, is Reimarus' account of Jesus' career, and all subsequent portrayals of Jesus as the revolutionary may be regarded as variations on the same theme. Such portrayals are used to uphold the argument that Jesus would support violent insurrections against unjust régimes.

Obviously this account of Jesus is completely at variance with the one which was used to support the pacifist position. Both cannot be correct. Interpreters have a habit of reading their own beliefs into Jesus, and then producing him as the authority for these beliefs, and this subjective element in the portraits of Jesus was one of the major factors that discredited the nineteenth-century attempts to produce biographies of the so-called historical Jesus. But is there any way of discriminating among the portraits? Is it all a matter of subjective preference? If this were the case, then Jesus and his teaching would be of no importance at all, for anyone could make of it what he wanted.

Actually, in the case we are considering at the moment, the great weight both of evidence and of scholarship lies against those who think of Jesus as a violent revolutionary. His expulsion of the traders from the Temple is an isolated event in his career which in any case is very far from having the character of an armed revolt. Violence would be in flat contradiction to his teaching and out of character with most of what we know about him. His followers, as we have noted, did not use violence, and this is probably due to what they had learned from Jesus himself. It is possible that Judas Iscariot among the disciples was a violent revolutionary, and one of the most likely reasons for his betrayal of Jesus was his disappointment when he discovered that Jesus did not intend to use violent means.

Jesus was unquestionably a radical and an opponent of the political and ecclesiastical establishment of his time, and his radicalism flowed inevitably from his strong eschatological convictions. But, as Johannes Weiss has put it, 'to hope for the kingdom of God in the transcendent sense of Jesus and to undertake revolution are as different as fire and water'.[11] Jesus was in fact too much of a radical to use the weapons of the existing order and so allow himself and his followers to get locked into the circle of violence. He chose, as we have seen, the more costly path of atonement. We have still to explore the meaning of this more fully, but among other things it means a radical change in values, whereas violence can only confirm the existing values and postpone any real change. Robert Evans, an interpreter of the so-called counter culture, makes a similar point with respect to our own times. 'The new revolutionaries,' he declares, 'are good sons of the technocracy.'[12] They are interested not in what Evans calls 'a new mind-set' but only in a transfer of power, and thus they are both the products and the preservers of the very system which they seek to overthrow. Theodore Roszak, another exponent of the counter culture, judges that 'revolutionary terrorism is only the mirror image of capitalist exploitation'. He sees as 'the greatest single victory bourgeois society has won over even its most irreconcilable opponents' the fact that 'it has inculcated in them its own shallow, reductionist image of man'.[13]

The root problem of violence is that it treats persons as less than persons, and also that it always leads to more violence as it progressively dehumanizes – or almost always does so. It imprisons those who practise it in a circle which keeps bringing them around once more to square one. Long before the Christian era, Aeschylus depicted this circle of violence in his tragedy *Agamemnon*, which shows how each deed of violence issues in another yet more terrible and destroys the humanity of those who participate in it. But it is Christianity which takes a further step and preaches a gospel of atonement and reconciliation whereby the chain of violence may be broken. 'Choosing different means, seeking another kind of victory, renouncing the marks of victory – this is the only possible way of breaking the chain of violence, of rupturing the circle of fear and hate,' writes Jacques Ellul.[14] Incidentally, Ellul offers perhaps the best criticism that is to be found of those Christians who have hastened to embrace violence as a means of social change. Ellul acknowledges their concern with social justice and the problem of poverty. But he finds them 'of a distressingly simplistic cast of mind'. They miss the complexities of the problem and see things only in a one-sided way. But what is worse still, their Christianity is one-sided, for they are finally not interested in reconciliation.

The problem is indeed a very difficult one and there are no simple solutions that can be applied automatically in every situation – neither absolute non-violence on the one hand nor a hasty resort to violence on the other. One of the few Christian writers who has wrestled with the problem in all its complexity is black theologian J. Deotis Roberts in a book with the significant title *Liberation and Reconciliation*. As a Christian, he believes that the ultimate goal must always be reconciliation. Yet he insists equally that there can be no true reconciliation until there has been liberation, a breaking of oppressions which may involve a sharpening of conflict and a temporary heightening of alienation, but which leads eventually to the liberation not only of the oppressed but of the oppressors. 'There can,' he says, 'be no shortcut to reconciliation that does not pass through liberation.'[15] In the light of all that we have learned already about the dynamic nature of peace and the creative role of conflict, we can readily recognize the truth of his words.

But we have still to answer the agonizing question of when and in what circumstances the resort to violence may be necessary even to the Christian. Are there any guidelines that can be offered? I suggest that we can get considerable help by looking at the traditional teaching of Christian moral theologians on the subject of the just war. It is often said nowadays that the doctrine of the just war has become quite obsolete. This is no doubt true if one is thinking of international wars, waged on the grand scale with nuclear weapons and the like. Such wars have introduced a kind of destruction which is not only quantitatively but qualitatively different from anything visualized by the moral theologians of former times, and which bursts through the bounds of their theories. But the doctrine of the just war still has an applicability to the type of violence we have been considering in this chapter.

The doctrine of the just war has a long history. It received its classic formulation at the hands of St Thomas Aquinas,[16] but it has been elaborated and expanded by other writers. I shall myself mention six conditions that have to be fulfilled, and these, I think, provide a sixfold test of the legitimacy of violence from a Christian point of view. The six conditions are:

1. There must be a just cause
2. Violence is the only way left of effecting change
3. There must be a properly constituted authority
4. There must be a feasible goal
5. The means must be appropriate to the end
6. Reconciliation is sought as the ultimate end.

Before commenting on these six points, let me just say a word about the expression 'just war'. It is an unfortunate expression, if it is understood in any sense other than a minimal and negative one. Historian Edward Gibbon was right when he wrote that 'war in its fairest form implies a perpetual violation of humanity and justice'.[17] There is no such thing as a 'holy war' – that, indeed, is the height of madness and blasphemy. We can speak of a just war only in the sense that sometimes in this distorted world there will be found conditions so degrading and dehumanizing that to leave them unchecked would be an even greater evil than to employ the violence of war for their removal.

The first of our six conditions was that there must be a just cause. Unquestionably there are many just causes in the world today. Millions of people are living under conditions of oppression and injustice. Millions of others have been driven from their homes and their livelihoods, and the refugee camp has become all too common a feature of life in our time, and a symbol of hopelessness. Such a camp brings home vividly, as perhaps nothing else does, the uprootedness, alienation, frustration that have been the lot of so many in our time. It is the very opposite of that fulfilled existence which is properly called peace. There is no question either that only unrelenting struggle and pressure will ever correct the conditions that have produced these human tragedies. But while these very conditions provide a breeding ground for violence, is it only the pressure of violent reaction that can alter them?

This question brings us to our second condition – that violence must be the last resort. There must be struggle and pressure, but only when every other avenue is barred may the struggle become violent. Unfortunately there is a tendency to hasten to the use of violence long before it can be legitimately considered as a last resort. Only when all other means have been used to the fullest extent – legal, political and non-violent pressures – could there be, from the point of view of Christian moral theology, any excuse for violence. This means that violence is never justified in states where legal and political channels are open, and where there is reasonable freedom of action. Only where every non-violent way of redress is denied can violence be considered acceptable.

The third condition for the use of violence is the demand that there must be some properly constituted authority to

direct the action. It is necessary here to bear in mind the circumstances in which this condition of the just war was first
formulated. It originated in the rough feudal period when
dukes and barons maintained private armies and there was
constant fighting of a purely sectional kind for the sake of private advantage. As against this chaotic proliferation of violence, the doctrine of the just war tried to limit the use of
physical force to legitimate governments. But this is one of the
most questionable features of the traditional doctrine. What
constitutes a legitimate government? Not just the actual pos-
session of power but, as John Locke saw, the consent of the
governed. A government may be established in power, but if
it is governing tyrannously, its claim to legitimacy may be
called in question. The complaint has been made, and probably with some justice, that Christian moral theology has too
often favoured the established powers. Great stress has been
laid on Paul's teaching about the 'powers that be' and his
belief that these powers derive their authority from God.
'For,' he writes, 'there is no authority except from God, and
those that exist have been instituted by God. Therefore he
who resists the authorities resists what God has appointed.'[18]
But this cannot be taken to mean that there ought never to
be resistance, even perhaps violent resistance, to a government that has forfeited its rights and lost the consent of the
people. It can be argued that a resistance movement enjoying
the confidence of a sizeable proportion of the population has
thereby become a legitimate authority. But it must be
stressed once more that the case for the use of violence would
be one that can very rarely be made out. No merely private
group is entitled to use violence to tear down the political
structure, and it should be remembered that of all the forms
of war and violence, civil disorder is the worst and rarely
achieves that freedom at which it aims. 'In the tumult of civil
discord,' wrote Gibbon, 'the laws of society lose their force

and their place is seldom supplied by those of humanity.'[19]

The fourth condition is that there must be a feasible goal. This rules out the' nihilistic and anarchic types of violence which seek only to tear down and destroy. Such forms of violence correspond to suicide in an individual. They amount to a total denial of hope and a total surrender to the evil of a situation which they despair of bettering. But only where there is the possibility of bettering the situation is any violence tolerable. Otherwise it can be nothing more than the final futility.

The fifth condition is that the means must be appropriate to the end, or proportionate to the end. The end certainly cannot be held to justify any means, especially if that end is peace or wholeness, for the end itself is affected and shaped by the means. We have taken note already that violence usually leads to more violence and defers peace to a still more distant future. Especially the indiscriminate violence and terrorist acts that have become so common today are bound to be inimical to the cause of peace. But one must not rule out the possibility that on some rare occasions a restrained use of force or a limited violence may be appropriate.

The last point is that from a Christian point of view any temporary resort to violence must look beyond the violent act to reconciliation. This is a point at which Christianity would sharply diverge from, let us say, Marxism. For even if both were convinced that an act of liberation had become imperative, Christianity would look finally to wholeness for both oppressed and oppressor – and this is implicit in the very notion of wholeness – whereas Marxism and many other revolutionary movements of a secular kind are concerned only to eliminate the oppressor. The essentially Christian character of the black theology of J. Deotis Roberts is shown by the fact that while he rightly claims that there can be no reconciliation that has not passed through liberation, yet reconciliation is the only ultimate goal acceptable to the Christian.

Our consideration of the six points based on the just war theory have made it plain that only very rarely indeed is a resort to violence justified – certainly from a Christian point of view, and perhaps from any humanitarian point of view. Violence is too often just the expression of ruthlessness. But the door does seem to have been left open for that very rare occasion when violence is justified. Is this only a theoretical possibility, mentioned perhaps as a palliative to those who might suspect that the preaching of peace is intended to lull them into quiescence and acquiescence? Or is it possible to cite a concrete example from recent times where the application of the criteria does seem to indicate that even from a Christian point of view revolutionary violence can be justified?

I think I can point to such a concrete case, and we may still have much to learn from it. But it is important to remember that the application of moral criteria to determine whether a course of action is justified is by no means so simple and unambiguous a matter as, let us say, testing the acidity of a liquid with a piece of litmus paper.

The case I have in mind is that of Dietrich Bonhoeffer, to whom brief allusion has already been made. Bonhoeffer has become the great Christian hero of the late twentieth century, and it is perhaps not surprising that in this time of violence, that hero is a man who believed it his Christian duty to take part in a conspiracy aimed at the violent overthrow of the German government at a time when Germany was engaged in warfare with an alliance of powerful nations.

At first glance, Bonhoeffer does not strike one as a likely person to engage in action directed towards assassination and the violent seizure of political power. He had been brought up in comfortable middle-class circumstances. He had a mild temperament. He was devoted to the church and was a man of deep piety. The Sermon on the Mount had a central place in his understanding of Christian discipleship. Theologically, he understood God not so much as ruler as one who shared the world's suffering. Yet finally it did seem to him that the way of discipleship led him into the dark and dangerous courses which brought him to the gallows.

How does his action appear in the light of the tests outlined above? Clearly, there was a just cause – half of Europe was under a despotic rule and Germany itself was being destroyed. Again, violence was the last resort, for with such ruthless rulers as those of Nazi Germany any non-violent resistance would have been crushed and no legal or political remedies remained. On the difficult question of whether there was a constituted authority to direct the violent action, it might be replied first that by its actions the Nazi government had forfeited all right to be regarded as the legitimate power in Germany, and second that the conspirators against Hitler numbered among them sufficient men of eminence that they could not be dismissed as a mere gang or clique but had the potentiality for becoming a government enjoying the consent of the people. Was there a feasible goal, a chance of success? Actually, Bonhoeffer and the others failed, and failed more than once. But on one occasion they did come pretty close to a possible success, and even up to the middle of 1944 their cause was never quite hopeless. Did they use means proportionate to the end? Their principal step toward the seizure of power was to have been the assassination of Hitler, and they were not equipped for any large-scale violence. Surely it could be argued that an act of violence against the dictator and perhaps some further acts against his immediate associates would be justified if it could halt or shorten the war and save many thousands of lives. Finally, these men did look beyond the immediate violent action to reconciliation both within Germany and beyond.

Was Bonhoeffer then justified in what he did? I think so. But on these moral questions there is always some ambiguity.

As Christians and as human beings we have to take the risk of moral action amid the ambiguities of life. It is impossible to say unequivocally that there was no better way than the one Bonhoeffer took or that his action can be totally justified. But it does seem clear that what would have been wrong on his part would have been to refuse the ambiguous decision and do what so many of his fellow-citizens and fellow-churchmen were doing – that is to say, nothing at all in the face of what was happening. As against their non-action, Bonhoeffer's action is justified a thousand times over.

NOTES

1. Roger L. Shinn, *Wars and Rumours of War*, Abingdon Press 1972, p. 274.
2. Op. cit., p.187.
3. Matt. 5.39-41 and 44.
4. Rom. 12.21.
5. G. Kaufman, *Systematic Theology: A Historicist Perspective*, Scribner 1968, p.219.
6. D. Bonhoeffer, *Letters and Papers from Prison*, The Enlarged Edition, SCM Press 1972, p.360.
7. Augustine, *Letters*, clxxxix, 4.
8. Rom. 13.1ff.
9. Bertrand Russell, *Autobiography*, Allen & Unwin 1967–69, vol. II, p.192.
10. Samuel Reimarus, *Fragments*, tr. R.S. Fraser, SCM Press 1971.
11. Johannes Weiss, *Jesus' Proclamation of the Kingdom of God*, SCM Press 1971, p.103.
12. R.A. Evans, *Belief and the Counter Culture*, Westminster Press 1971, p.32.
13. Theodore Roszak, *The Making of a Counter Culture*, Faber 1970, pp.58, 100.
14. Jacques Ellul, *Violence*, tr. C.G. Kings, SCM Press 1970, p.173.
15. J. Deotis Roberts, *Liberation and Reconciliation: A Black Theology*, Westminster Press 1971, p.191.
16. Thomas Aquinas, *S. Th.*, II, ii; q.40.

17. Edward Gibbon, *Decline and Fall of the Roman Empire*, abridged D.M. Low, Chatto and Windus 1960, p.474.

18. Rom. 13.1f.

19. Op. cit., p.47.

FIVE

The Metaphysics of Peace

Some people may feel slightly shocked by the title of this chapter. The word 'metaphysics' has not been popular in recent times, and I cannot expect that it will be a popular move to claim that the concept of peace is finally a metaphysical one. But perhaps when I explain in more detail what I mean by a metaphysical concept some of the initial suspicion may be overcome. By a metaphysical concept, I mean one the boundaries of which cannot be precisely determined, not because we lack information but because the concept itself turns out to have such depth and inexhaustibility that the more we explore it, the more we see that something further remains to be explored. The more we grasp it, the more we become aware that it extends beyond our grasp. Those who have an implacable hostility to the metaphysical might find it easier to speak of peace as a mystery. For a mystery is not something that just cannot be understood, but something that, the more clearly it is understood, reveals a breadth or a height or a depth that stretches beyond the limits of understanding.

I am not referring merely to the multi-dimensional character of peace, though we have seen that when the concept is considered in any depth, it reaches into every major area of human life. There can be no peace in the fullest sense of a wholeness, dignity and freedom for all men unless many areas of life – political, social, racial, economic, personal and so on

— are transformed, and in such a way that the several transformations all interlock with each other. But this is a question of complexity rather than of metaphysics or mystery, and at least in large part it belongs to the technique of peace rather than to a philosophical or theological concept of peace. I will not say, however, that the multi-dimensional character of peace is quite unrelated to its metaphysical character. The very fact that metaphysics have been despised in recent times has contributed to the fragmentary way in which life has been understood. If today we are understanding that techniques cannot be applied in isolation and that we need to establish among them such relations as will make them mutually supportive and avoid undesirable side-effects, then we have at least taken a step towards trying to see things in their wholeness and interrelatedness, that is to say, synthetically as well as analytically. If peace in turn is fundamentally wholeness, and if metaphysics seeks to maximize our perception of wholeness and interrelatedness, then peace and metaphysics may be more closely linked than is sometimes supposed; while, conversely, the fragmented understanding of life may well be connected with the actual fracturing of life itself, a fracturing which is the opposite of peace.

But the true metaphysical dimensions of peace emerge because even to seek a wholeness for human life drives us to ask questions which take us to the very boundaries of understanding. What is finally of value? What is real and what is illusory? What conditions would one need to postulate as making possible the realization of a true peace?

It is when we begin to expose ourselves to such questions — and they can scarcely be avoided if we take the question of peace with the utter seriousness which it demands — that we can also begin to understand the meaning of some words of St Paul when he writes to the Christian disciples: 'The peace of God, which passes all understanding, will keep your hearts and minds in Christ Jesus.'[1] 'The peace of God' — the use of God-language here indicates that peace is an ultimate; it 'passes all understanding' — that is to say, it stretches beyond the limits of everything material, empirical, manipulable. If Paul seems too much the religious enthusiast, let me set alongside his words another quotation from a very secular devotee of peace, Bertrand Russell. Recalling the time that he spent in China, he tells us: 'We usually spent the whole day in the Temple of Heaven, the most beautiful building that it has ever been my good fortune to see. We would sit in the winter sunshine, saying little, gradually absorbing peace, and would come away prepared to face the madness and passion of our own distracted continent with poise and calm.'[2] However one may seek to explain it, the very essence of peace seems to be something that we absorb, something that comes like a gift in the very depth of our being. Again we may remember Christ's words: 'Peace I leave with you, my peace I give unto you.'[3] Let me not be misunderstood at this point. I do not wish to seem for a moment to depreciate the vital importance of technical knowledge as a way to peace, and I do not wish to play down the labour and struggle on the road to peace — indeed, I have laid great stress on these matters throughout this book. But these alone do not and cannot constitute the whole of peace. There is still more to peace, and though this 'more' may be elusive, it cannot be ignored.

Peace implies not just the application of techniques on a vast complex scale, not just the remaking of social and political structures, but a profound change in the depths of man himself. There must be a reordering of priorities and a transvaluation of values. Even some Marxist philosophers nowadays recognize that a change in social structures can achieve little unless there is a reshaping of man's nature. Herbert Marcuse, for instance, visualizes a society 'in which a different type of human being will have emerged, a man with a new sensibility and sensitivity."⁴ This sounds very much like a religious demand, and it is hard to see that traditional Marxism had any resources for coping with it.

But what, again, do we mean by the remaking or transformation of human nature? It cannot be meant that man is to become something other than man. On the contrary. As I understand this expression, I mean that man should become man for the first time. Man as we have known him in the harshly competitive societies of the modern world is not truly man, but a distortion. But once man has fallen away from himself and his life has become distorted, how can he ever find the way to himself? How can he become that remade or transformed being who will transcend the ways of selfish competition and live constructively on the level of co-operation and mutual help? Pessimists have often said that you cannot change human nature. This is a given. Man did not choose it in the first instance; he found himself living with it. But if the true nature of man is better described by Locke than by Hobbes – as we decided in an earlier chapter⁵ – then it is this true nature which is the fundamental given. This may be the reason for finding both religious and secular writers describing peace as somehow a gift, to be accepted or absorbed, for it means in this sense accepting ourselves, accepting what is most fundamentally *given* in our humanity, though in actual life this given is distorted and covered up by the innumerable sins into which men fall. In the pursuit of peace we are summoned to engage in many active enterprises, but within them all and beyond them all we are being asked to accept what man truly is. We are being asked to give free course to a wholeness that is already part of the gift of being.

We can arrive at the same truths from the opposite direction, that is to say, by way of a negative approach. In the first chapter,⁶ we spent some time considering the many ways in which human life is fractured, and we discussed briefly the phenomenon of alienation. The very word 'alienation' means 'becoming other', so that when we talk of alienation in human life, we are implicitly recognizing that there is a more fundamental form of humanity from which the many alienated forms are deviations. No one could have the sense of alienation unless there were in him a still deeper sense of wholeness which he felt to have been violated. Now alienation too is a metaphysical idea if we probe it to its furthest limits. Beyond all the relative forms of alienation which are studied in the behavioural and human sciences, there is the sense of being alienated from the whole scheme of things. This deep-lying alienation is the final threat to peace, indeed, the final threat to any meaningful interpretation of human life. This deep onto-logical alienation, as we have noted,[7] has been characteristic of modern times, yet like every other form of alienation it points beyond itself to a more fundamental mode of wholeness. This wholeness too may be described as ontological. Sociologist Peter Berger gives an illustration of what I have in mind. He pictures a child, waking up in the dark. There are no familiar objects visible, 'the contours of trusted reality are blurred', as Berger expresses it. The child cries out. The mother comes to comfort him. She will probably say something like, 'Don't be afraid, everything is in order, everything is all right.' Berger points out that trivial though such an incident may seem, it has far-reaching implications. To say '*everything* is in order' is to make a metaphysical asser-tion. Let me quote his words. 'The formula can, without in any way violating it, be translated into a statement of cosmic scope – "Have trust in being!" ' He concludes: 'At the very centre of the process of becoming fully human, at the core of *humanitas*, we find an experience of trust in the order of reality.'[8]

Of course, one may at once ask whether this experience of trust may not be just a wish projection, arising from the need for security, and Berger's own illustration of the child awaking in the dark lends point to the question. On the other hand, one might argue that it is logically impossible to experience alienation apart from a prior sense of belonging, which alienation contradicts, so that it is experienced as that which should not be. The face of the world itself is ambiguous, and in different ages of mankind or even at different periods in the life of the same individual, alienation or belonging, anxiety or peace of mind, may be the predominant 'sense of life'. On theoretical grounds alone, it is probably impossible to demonstrate conclusively that the one attitude or the other is better founded in 'the way things are'. Here we are reminded of the similar ambiguity that attended the question whether war or peace is the 'natural state' of man, and here again we have to be reminded that this is no purely factual question, for the answer which we give determines our practical attitudes and so helps to mould the reality itself.

The relation between our deepest convictions (whether or not one wishes to call these 'metaphysical') and our practical attitudes is no doubt a reciprocal one, but it has considerable importance in shaping human life. In Camus' novel *La Peste* a priest and a doctor find themselves fighting together against an outbreak of plague in an Algerian city. The priest says to the doctor, who is a sceptic: 'I see that you too are working for the salvation of mankind.' The doctor replies: 'That is not quite correct. Salvation is too big a word for me. I am working first of all for man's health.' Up to a point, the doctor's reply is justified, for it is easy to make such a theological notion as 'salvation' something so remote and spiritualized that we may even make it an excuse for overlooking the down to earth things that lie to hand and that are quite indispensable to man's wholeness. Yet the priest has his point also. For health, like peace, has to do with wholeness, and the more one explores in depth the meaning of health, the more it becomes clear that this too is an idea with fluid boundaries. To think of health as freedom from germs is only a crude and inadequate first approximation to the meaning — as crude and inadequate as the understanding of peace as the absence of war. The notion of health goes on to consider man in relation to his environment, his social and economic conditions, the life of the mind and spirit of man as well as of his body. This does not mean that the concrete manageable problems of health are lost to view in some vague conception of human well-being, but it does mean that the concrete problems are seen in a wider context and in relation to many other problems; and often it will be the case that one problem or group of problems cannot be solved without a simultaneous attack on related problems, or again that the solution of one problem in isolation may produce undesirable results if other interlocking problems have been neglected. To go back for a moment to my illustration from the novel of Camus, I am simply saying that if the priest had made preoccupation with a metaphysical idea of salvation an excuse for avoiding the practical problems of the suffering community, then he needed the rebuke of the doctor; but if the doctor was absorbed in a positivist concern with the matter immediately to hand, he needed the priest's vision of man in the totality of his needs so that he could understand his task in a wider context. So it is in the case of peace. There are the immediate tasks, the urgent situations, the obvious concrete needs, and there are practical ways of responding to these. But even on the practical level our responses are influenced and motivated by wider considerations about who man is and wherein his true well-being consists. To probe the meaning of peace in any depth and to pursue the realization of peace with any sense of direction drive us to consider those ulterior implicates of peace, implicates which may fairly be called metaphysical or theological.

Let me now consider three ideas which have been important

in Christian theology and all of which have relevance to the understanding of peace. Taken together, they deepen our understanding of what peace essentially is and at the same time provide a background of conviction which should strengthen human efforts toward peace. The three ideas are grace, atonement and resurrection.

Although I have not used the word 'grace' in earlier discussions, something closely akin to this idea was present in our talk about the 'given' in human life. In theology, the word 'grace' refers to that which is freely given, to that which comes like a gift to man from beyond himself. The experience of grace is the experience of finding our human strivings towards a more authentically human life borne up and supported by a reality beyond ourselves and even beyond human society in its totality. It is the experience of belonging to and working with a creative drive towards a wholeness and integrity that go beyond man's best aspirations. What is implied in this experience of grace is a deep affinity between man and his ideals on the one hand and that vast non-human reality within which human life has its setting on the other. What is the character of that non-human reality? Is it sub-human or superhuman? Is it a faceless, lifeless, mechanistic universe, as nineteenth-century science tended to conceive it, essentially indifferent or even hostile to human aspirations, so that the ideal of peace is a very precarious one that has to be pursued in the face of forces that are all the time working against it? Or is the physical universe but the visible expression of a deeper reality having affinity with man in his personal and spiritual being, a reality for which peace or wholeness also counts and which is supportive of its realization? It is in this second way that the Bible has understood man's place in the world, God being the personal, historical, cosmic power seeking to realize wholeness in his creation, while man is his co-worker. And where man pursues war rather than peace, he frustrates himself and comes into collision with reality, for peace, not war, is the primordial reality. 'The stars in their courses fought against Sisera,' as an Old Testament writer expressed it, admittedly in terms of a mythological astralism.[9] I think that today, even if there is a reluctance to use the traditional God-language, there is a move in the direction of rediscovering man's affinity with a wider reality, the affinity which was denied in the days of mechanistic materialism and similar points of view. Poets and novelists are seeking for it. But scientists also are stressing man's belonging in the universe, as against that nineteenth-century view which saw only a desperate struggle for existence in the face of hostile forces. Consider these words of Barbara Jackson and Rene Dubos: 'There is something clarifying and irresistible in plain scientific fact. The astonishing thing about our deepened understanding of reality over the last four or five decades is the degree to which it confirms and reinforces so many of the older moral insights of man. The philosophers told us we were one, part of a greater unity which transcends our local drives and needs. They told us that all living things are held together in a most intricate web of interdependence. They told us that aggression and violence, blindly breaking down the delicate relationships of existence, could lead to destruction and death. These were, if you like, intuitions, drawn in the main from the study of human societies and behaviour. What we now learn is that they are factual descriptions of the way in which our universe actually works.'[10] To be sure, they are talking about the natural world, as we have learned about it from physics, biology and other sciences. But this conception of the world as a unified harmonious system, life producing, life supporting, life enhancing, readily lends itself to something akin to a theistic interpretation, for it implies that reason and order, even love and peace, are characteristic of reality. Convictions of this kind supply a rationale for peace and are a powerful encouragement towards its pursuit.

The second idea to be considered is that of atonement. We have already noted that atonement and reconciliation have a central place in Christian thought, differentiating it from such alternatives as Marxism.[11] The idea of atonement is a complex one, and always includes two strands. The first is that of reconciliation – to atone is to make at one, to bring together in a unity persons who for one reason or another had become estranged. But there is a second strand of meaning, that of cost or suffering on the part of the one who makes the atonement; it would seem that when a unity has been breached, it can be renewed again only through some price being paid. Jesus Christ himself is the one who effects atonement. His whole life is given to the work of reconciliation, but the climax of that work is constituted by his death and sufferings, which are seen as the price of reconciliation. The new reconciled community which he brought into existence and in which Jew and Gent-ile, hitherto alienated from each other, now met in friendship, confessed that Christ is 'our peace' and in particular they attributed the reconciliation to 'the blood of Christ'.[12] Only a costly act of atonement could break out of that vicious circle of violence which perpetuates enmity from generation to generation and of which there are so many tragic examples in world history, including the history of our own times. But this atoning work of Christ is not to be seen as an isolated act. The reconciled community which he called into being is itself to be a reconciling community, continuing his ministry of reconciliation and continuing to pay the cost of it. And if this seems an impossibly hard demand on the Christian commun-ity – and admittedly it has fulfilled it only in very erratic and imperfect ways – we have to remember that atonement has to be seen in relation to grace. For to the extent that the Chris-tian community has been able to follow Christ in the way of costly reconciliation, this has depended on the belief that

Christ in his atoning work reveals God himself. This in turn means that costly atonement is built into the very texture of life. New and larger unities are built up as lesser unities permit themselves to be dissolved. Yet this happens in such a way that differences are preserved and the new unity is richer because of the differences. If this language sounds somewhat Hegelian, it is because Hegel grasped the universal character of atonement very well. 'That the concrete act (of sacrifice) may be possible,' he argued, 'the absolute Being must have from the start implicitly sacrificed itself.'[13] Christians would express this by saying that there has been a cross in God from the beginning. And those who have grasped this may find it less difficult themselves to take up the cross and join in the work of atonement.

The third theological idea is that of resurrection. Christ's crucifixion did not mean that he was got rid of – on the contrary, his reconciling work continued with new vigour and now extended throughout a whole community. The basic idea of resurrection is that life is stronger than death, that man never finds himself in a dead end but that always a new possibility opens up. This is not a blind optimism. It is once again a metaphysical conviction, closely related to the ideas of grace and atonement. Resurrection adds the eschatological dimension. It is the belief that man's life and indeed all history has a direction and moves towards a goal. We have seen that peace in the full sense is an eschatological idea.[14] It cannot be completely realized in history. In fact, the pursuit of peace has been so often frustrated and peace even at its more provisional levels has proved so elusive that it is easy to become sceptical about it. But if there is a goal to history, if there is the possibility of that radical kind of renewal which is called resurrection, then peace does lie within the range of possibility, and it would seem that only if it lies within this range can it engage men's serious endeavours and call forth the sacrifices which the universal law of atonement demands.

I have related peace to three ideas which are of importance in Christian theology, though it should be noted that they have a place in many religious faiths. The truth of these ideas cannot be demonstrated, but it may be claimed that they are entirely compatible with what we know of human life and that they do not lack support in human experience. But when we consider them in relation to peace, perhaps what we must say about them is what Kant said about God, freedom and immortality in relation to the moral life – namely, that they are postulates. If one takes peace seriously in all its depth of meaning, then it seems to carry with it some such postulates as those I have mentioned. As a fulfilled state of humanity, peace postulates an end or goal of history transcending all the provisional goals that lie on the way to it, and is thus in its complete sense an eschatological ideal. Since the only way to the end lies through history, peace postulates an atoning work in history, for this alone can enable men to break out of the cycle of violence so that they may attain to a reconciled relationship. And since atonement and sacrifice run so counter to the selfishness and aggression of fallen man, peace postulates grace, for men will only rise above their fallenness to lay hands on their true humanity if they are drawn and supported by the creative power of reality itself – the power which the religions call God. Man is called to be the agent of peace, yet he is empowered to be the agent because he is also the instrument of peace, perhaps one of many instruments joined together in realizing a goal greater than any of us can imagine.

And that phrase, 'instrument of peace', recalls the famous prayer of St. Francis of Assisi, a prayer which sums up in a remarkable way all the many dimensions of the concept of peace and which we may fittingly use to close this chapter: 'Lord, make me an instrument of thy peace. Where there is hatred, let me sow love; where there is injury, pardon; where there is doubt, faith; where there is despair, hope; where there is sadness, joy; where there is darkness, light.'

NOTES

1. Phil. 4.7.

2. Bertrand Russell, *Autobiography*, Allen and Unwin 1967-69, vol. II, p.129.

3. John 14.27.

4. In *Marxism and Radical Religion*, ed. J.C. Raines and T. Dean, Temple University Press 1970, p.9.

5. See above, pp.26f.

6. See above, pp.3ff.

7. See above, pp.8f.

8. Peter Berger, *A Rumour of Angels*, Allen Lane: The Penguin Press, pp.68f.

9. Judg. 5.20.

10. Barbara Jackson and Rene Dubos, *Only One Earth*, Penguin Books 1972, p.85.

11. See above, p.58.

12. Eph. 2.13-14.

13. G.W.F. Hegel, *The Phenomenology of Mind*, tr. J.B. Baillie, Allen and Unwin 1930, p.722.

14. See above, p.17.

SIX

What is to be Done?

We have completed our exploration of the concept of peace, but it has been our intention from the beginning not to allow this exploration to become merely speculative or visionary but to serve as a guide to the intelligent pursuit of peace. So we cannot leave the subject without facing a question that must have arisen in the minds of most readers of the book: What is to be done? And most of these readers, we may assume, are not statesmen or men of great power and influence, but ordinary citizens.

Perhaps many of them feel that there is nothing that they can do. World affairs seem nowadays to be controlled by vast forces that no one quite understands so that statesmen themselves appear to be driven along courses which they do not willingly choose. We have lately seen two Presidents of the United States struggling vainly to extricate their country from a costly and unpopular war, yet apparently powerless to do so. If the most powerful men in the world are dragged along by forces too strong for them to control, what can ordinary citizens do?

This feeling of helplessness is not new. In his great novel, *War and Peace*, Leo Tolstoy was never tired of maintaining that in the wars that convulsed Europe in the early nineteenth century, individuals, even the great Napoleon himself, were entirely subordinate to vast collective currents — 'the mysterious forces that move humanity'. But another famous novelist saw the same events in a very different manner. In *Les Miserables* Victor Hugo depicts Napoleon as the great man who alters the course of history. 'The excessive weight of this man in human destiny disturbed the equilibrium.' But Hugo also believed in a providential power, an 'incorruptible supreme equity', which finally delivered history from the great man.

The forces shaping history are no doubt very complex and are largely not understood. But it is not just a matter of fate. Men, even ordinary men, have some part in shaping history. We come back to the problem of which we were already compelled to take cognizance in the opening pages of this book – the problem of the relation between the large-scale and the small-scale, the global life of man and the individual lives of men. Neither can be totally absorbed in the other. Individual lives are unquestionably shaped by vast collective movements, yet these movements derive their strength and motivation from the consent of individuals.

Thus, in the quest for peace, the strivings of individuals are not to be written off; and the more such individuals, the better. 'Personal morality and political and social institutions,' wrote F. H. Bradley, 'cannot exist apart, and (in general) the better the one, the better the other.'[1]

Let me then set down in summary form a few of the ways in which concerned individuals can contribute towards the global virtue of peace. These suggestions are all fairly obvious, but unless enough people take them seriously, it is hard to see how there can be a true peace.

1. *Be an agent of reconciliation* in those situations of conflict which impinge on your own life – and surely nowadays almost everyone is caught up in some situation of conflict, whether international or racial or industrial or something else. But how does one help towards reconciliation in such situations? It is not done by glossing over the differences, for we

have seen that these have to be brought into the open. What is necessary is to maintain communication. When people can talk together even about their differences, there is often remarkable progress towards a fair resolution of the conflict. On the other hand, when communication has broken down, peace has been made inaccessible. The value of communication was brought home to me very forcibly when I lived for some years in New York in a racially sensitive area where a middle-class white district touches the edge of black Harlem. The two racial communities existed side by side with the minimum of communication and each fearful and suspicious of the other. It was only after some months that I discovered a local church where members of both communities were meeting together with the barriers down and were working together for the benefit of the whole neighbourhood. That church and others like it were performing an inestimable service to the city in promoting peace. If only that kind of dialogue could take place in all situations of conflict, then the world would be much closer to a true peace.

I need hardly remind the reader of how this theme of the reconciling power of dialogue received classic statement by one of the great prophets of this century, Martin Buber. In an essay entitled 'Genuine Dialogue and the Possibilities of Peace', he declared that the absence of such dialogue 'is not only the most acute symptom of the pathology of our time, it is also that which most urgently makes a demand of us'. But what is genuine dialogue? According to Buber, it takes place when 'each of the partners, even when he stands in opposition to the other, heeds, affirms, and confirms his opponent as an existing other; only so can conflict certainly not be eliminated from the world, but be humanly arbitrated and led toward its overcoming'.[2] To take part in such dialogue, then, I see as one contribution that the concerned person can make towards realizing peace.

2. *Be politically and socially responsible.* In the highly organized and institutionalized world in which we live, the efforts of individuals will be unavailing unless ways can be found to shape and influence the powerful and apparently depersonalized political, economic and social forces that determine the large-scale structures of human life. Most of us can find access at one point or another to organizations that have some share in shaping society – political parties, local government bodies, trade unions, educational associations and so on. But to get oneself seriously involved in any of these demands time, commitment and responsibility, such as few may be willing to invest. It is so much easier to take part in a demonstration, and leave it at that! But it is only the less spectacular but steady engagement with the problems of society that will in the long run help to bring us towards a genuine peace.

For in politics nowadays as in social conflicts between entrenched groups there seems to be increasing polarization. This in effect means that the conflicts become hard and impersonal, each side simply trying to enforce its will on the other. To serve the cause of peace in such situations is to try to humanize the thought and action of these social groups. This is certainly not easy, for it is notorious that groups are swayed by self-interest and pursue their self-interest with a ruthlessness that usually goes far beyond that of individuals. But though it is not easy, it is not impossible. Certainly the peace lover has a duty to try to bring some compassion and understanding into these conflicts. Richard Holloway, who has spent many years serving the cause of peace and social justice, has written: 'In an age in which politics is increasingly characterized by hatred and a carefully articulated intolerance, the Christian can participate only in the spirit of pity.'[3] What he says about the Christian would, of course, apply to other lovers of peace. Their participation in these areas is needed if political and social action is to be saved from dehumanization and made to serve the cause of wholeness for all, that is to say, the cause of a genuine and lasting peace.

3. *Exercise restraint in your material standard of living.* This is not easy in the affluent countries of the world. All the pressures are upon us to increase production and consumption. The success of societies is measured by their gross national product. The traditional virtues of thrift and restraint have been turned into vices in the context of what Alvin Toffler has called 'the throw-away society'.[4] Acquisitiveness is encouraged, and where the total volume of goods keeps growing, it is presumably hoped that acquisitiveness need not turn into aggressiveness.

But perhaps the time has come when a moderate Christian asceticism has once again an important role to play as a witness to the belief that the fullness of human life does not consist simply in the abundance of material possessions and that in any case there is something fundamentally wrong with a situation in which some people in some nations degrade themselves through over-consumption while other people in other countries are degraded by not having anything more than a marginal level of physical subsistence. We have seen in an earlier discussion how man's war with nature tends to provoke international unrest.[5] This situation is likely to become more acute as certain natural resources become scarcer and scarcer. A continuation of the present glaring inequities in the different standards of living will remain a standing threat to peace, indeed, a constant frustration of peace if we understand peace in any affirmative way. Whether eventually a vastly improved technology will raise the standard of living of all to the levels now enjoyed by the affluent countries is doubtful, and whether it is desirable to turn the whole world into a kind of plush suburbia is even more doubtful. What is certain is that in the short term the standard of living of the poorer countries can only be raised if there is some voluntary restraint of consumption on the part of the richer countries. What also seems certain is that no political party in the affluent countries has the courage to ask the electorate to support a policy that would seek to reduce consumption – such a policy, we are told, would be political suicide. Thus it becomes necessary for individuals and voluntary groups to make their witness against the grosser forms of 'conspicuous consumption'. Though I have used the word 'asceticism', I am asking only for a simplicity of life style that will eschew unwarranted luxury and extravagance and that will consciously reject the ideals of the 'good life' based on the production and consumption of material goods.

4. *Pray for peace.* Though I mention this last, it is not in any sense an afterthought or an extra. Where people are praying for peace, the cause of peace is being strengthened by their very act of prayer, for they are themselves becoming immersed in the spirit of peace and committed to the cause of peace. In this broad sense of prayer, the non-Christian can with a good conscience join with his Christian brethren in praying for peace. This very book is in one sense a kind of extended prayer for peace, in so far as it is an attempt to reflect or meditate in at least some depth on the meaning of peace and to become caught up in the love and pursuit of peace.

But to pray for peace, Christians believe, is more than just to meditate on the meaning of peace with a view to becoming better servants of the cause of peace. It is to bring into the human situation the very power of the God of peace, or, better expressed, to open up our human situation to that power. No doubt at any given time only a tiny minority of mankind is actively praying for peace in this way. But no one can say what is being accomplished through the openings into the human situation which they provide. Those who pray for peace can take encouragement from some words in *The Cloud of Unknowing*: 'The whole of mankind is wonderfully helped by what you are doing, in ways you do not understand.'[6]

NOTES

1. F. H. Bradley, *Ethical Studies,* Oxford University Press 1927, p.188.
2. Martin Buber, *Pointing the Way,* tr. Maurice Friedman, Routledge and Kegan Paul 1957, p.238.
3. Richard Holloway, *Let God Arise,* Mowbray 1972, p.118.
4. Alvin Toffler, *Future Shock,* Bantam Books 1970, p.51.
5. See above, p.7.
6. *The Cloud of Unknowing,* ed. C. Wolters, Penguin Books 1961, p.53.